THE COLORS OF THE NEW WORLD

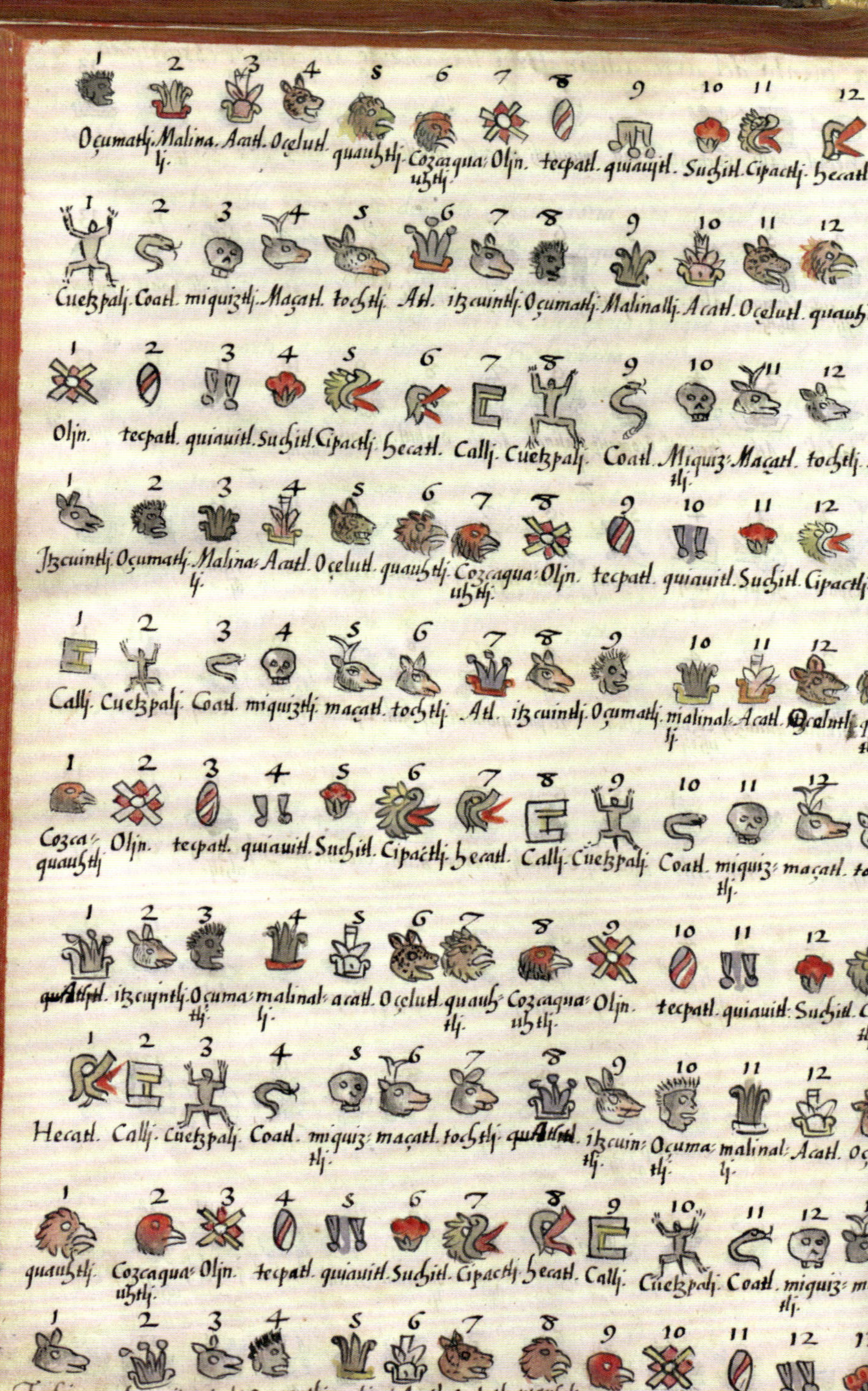
Oçumatli. Malina li. Acatl. Ocelutl. quauhtli. Coçaqua uhtli. Olin. tecpatl. quiauitl. Suchitl. Cipactli. hecatl. cal
Cuetzpali. Coatl. miquiztli. Maçatl. tochtli. Atl. itzcuintli. Oçumatli. Malinalli. Acatl. Ocelutl. quauhtli. qua uh tli
Olin. tecpatl. quiauitl. Suchitl. Cipactli. hecatl. Calli. Cuetzpali. Coatl. Miquiz tli. Maçatl. tochtli. At
Itzcuintli. Oçumatli. Malina li. Acatl. Ocelutl. quauhtli. Coçaqua uhtli. Olin. tecpatl. quiauitl. Suchitl. Cipactli. he
Calli. Cuetzpali. Coatl. miquiztli. maçatl. tochtli. Atl. itzcuintli. Oçumatli. malinal li. Acatl. Ocelutl. qua uh tli
Cozca quauhtli. Olin. tecpatl. quiauitl. Suchitl. Cipactli. hecatl. Calli. Cuetzpali. Coatl. miquiz. maçatl. toch tli
quauhtli. itzcuintli. Ocuma tli. malinal li. acatl. Ocelutl. quauh tli. Coçaqua uhtli. Olin. tecpatl. quiauitl. Suchitl. Cip tli
Hecatl. Calli. Cuetzpali. Coatl. miquiz. maçatl. tochtli. quauhtli. itzcuin tli. Ocuma tli. malinal li. Acatl. Oçe
quauhtli. Cozcaqua uhtli. Olin. tecpatl. quiauitl. Suchitl. Cipactli. hecatl. Calli. Cuetzpali. Coatl. miquiz. ma
Tochin itzcuintli. Oçumatli. malinal Acatl. Ocelutl. quauhtli. Cozcaqua. Olin. tecpatl. quiauitl. Suc

THE COLORS OF THE NEW WORLD

Artists, Materials, and the Creation of the *Florentine Codex*

Diana Magaloni Kerpel

GETTY RESEARCH INSTITUTE

**Getty Research Institute
Publications Program**

Thomas W. Gaehtgens, *Director,*
   Getty Research Institute
Gail Feigenbaum, *Associate Director*

The Getty Research Institute Council
generously supported this book.

The Colors of the New World publishes Diana
Magaloni Kerpel's lecture of the same title,
held at the Getty Center on 7 November 2013.

© 2014 J. Paul Getty Trust
Third printing

**Published by the Getty Research Institute,
Los Angeles**
Getty Publications
1200 Getty Center Drive, Suite 500
Los Angeles, California 90049-1682
getty.edu/publications

Laura Santiago, *Manuscript Editor*
Stacy Miyagawa, *Production Coordinator*
Jim Drobka, *Designer*

Diana Magaloni Kerpel's and Cuauhtémoc
Medina's texts were translated from the Spanish
by Debra Nagao.

Distributed in the United States and Canada
by the University of Chicago Press

Distributed outside the United States and
Canada by Yale University Press, London

Printed in China

Type composed in Clifford and Avenir

Library of Congress
Cataloging-in-Publication Data
Magaloni Kerpel, Diana, author.
   The colors of the new world : artists,
materials, and the creation of the Florentine
codex / Diana Magaloni Kerpel.
      pages cm
   Introductory essay by Cuauhtémoc Medina.
   Includes bibliographical references.
   ISBN 978-1-60606-329-3
1. Códice florentino. 2. Illumination of books
and manuscripts—Mexico—Technique.
3. Pigments. 4. Artists' materials—Mexico.
5. Manuscripts, Mex an. I. Medina,
Cuauhtémoc, writer of introduction. II. Title.
   F1219.56.C7552M34 2014
   751.2—dc23
                        2014001971

CONTENTS

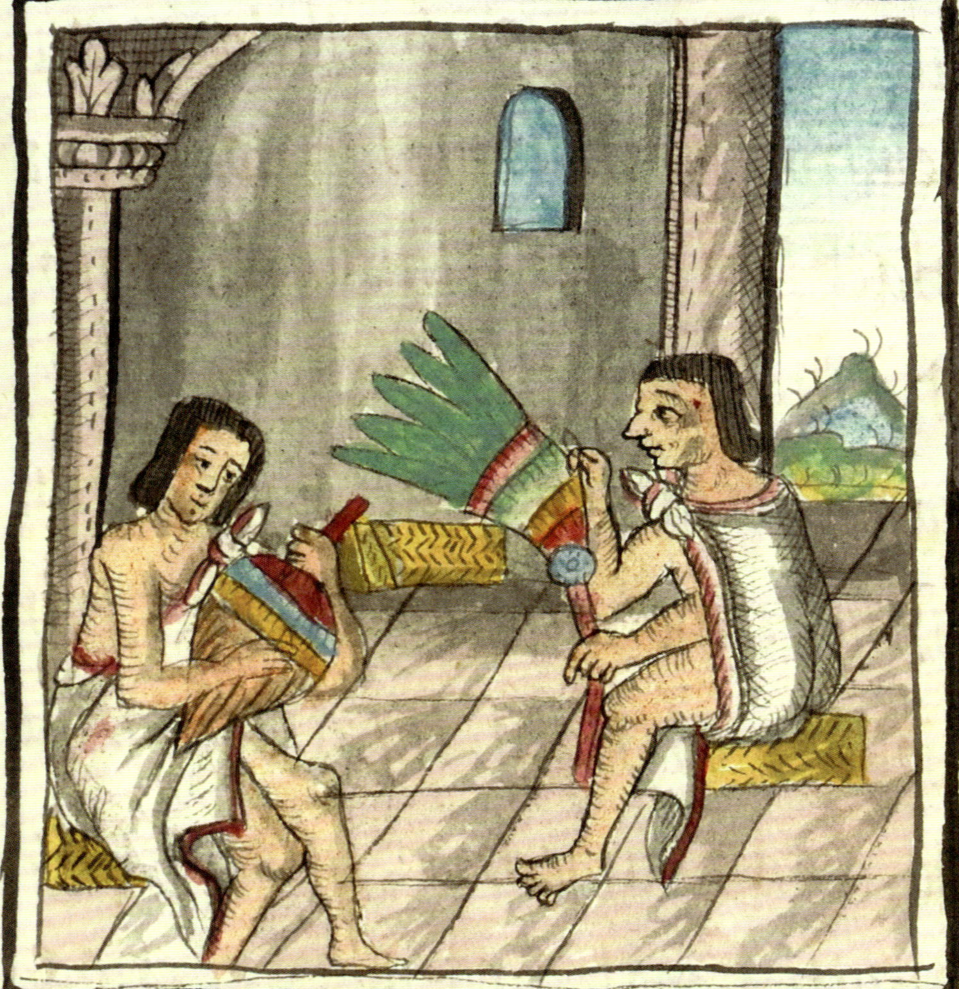

Diana Magaloni Kerpel is the first laureate of the Getty Research Institute Council Lecture Series: New Research in Art History. One of the world's leading art historians in the fields of pre-Columbian and Latin American colonial art, Magaloni Kerpel has forged an innovative approach to examining the visual culture of pre-Hispanic and early colonial Mexico. Her scholarly work is characterized by its agility in crossing barriers erected by academic disciplines.

A generation ago, the fields of art history and conservation science were relatively independent. Each field had its own concerns; rarely did the two join forces to consider specific problems. This is no longer true. A new generation of scholars has not only fostered greater exchange between the disciplines but also demonstrated the tremendous potential for critical insights into the creation and understanding of works of art arising from their joint pursuit.

Diana Magaloni Kerpel's investigations on the manuscript known as the *Florentine Codex,* which is held at the Laurentian Library in Florence, have transformed our knowledge of one of the salient manuscripts of the sixteenth century. Her work, carried out in concert with that of a team of scientists, anthropologists, and art historians, has revealed key aspects of the *Florentine Codex* itself as well as of a society at a time of profound change following the Spanish conquest of Mexico. Magaloni Kerpel's pioneering research on the codex is the subject of this book.

This publication and the lecture that preceded it are sponsored by the Getty Research Institute Council. The council supports the Getty Research Institute in bringing new scholarly research in art history to the attention of a larger public. It also shares the Research Institute's mission of broadening its geographic scope and making art-historical research material accessible around the globe.

Thomas W. Gaehtgens
Director, Getty Research
Institute

Brian Sweeney
Chair, Getty Research
Institute Council

The idea of the authority of historical or ethnographic documentary sources sounds deceptively natural to scholars who study the past of indigenous America. Nineteenth- and twentieth-century heuristics began with the assumption that historical information and testimonies passed freely from document to document, as the water in rivers flows from springs to slopes, to tributaries, and into the hands of researchers in the present. Thus, the flow of the history of indigenous peoples not only privileged (or postulated) an "original source" regarded as the most authentic but also—as an ancillary to the construction of modern studies—gave primacy in interpretation to whichever source was regarded as the closest to a primary document.

Behind its apparent neutrality, the concept of a documentary source is perhaps an imposition as problematic and Eurocentric for the study of the indigenous world as the very notion of "art." The modern conception of art served empires, states, academics, dealers, and collectors in stockpiling all sorts of trophies in their museums and collections as evidence of the demotion of epistemologies and ways of life; likewise, the idea that the production of the indigenous past in its highly diverse forms—that is, in its images, sculpture, architecture, and alphabetic texts—is comparable to a primary source for the ongoing universal narrative of history has subjected all of these original forms of communication to a definitive process of epistemic colonization. The authority of the written document in Western history has overshadowed the incredibly rich and creative manuscripts painted in the sixteenth century in New Spain that were the result of an unprecedented collaboration between indigenous and European authors. In these documents, artists tested a new way of recording by employing alphabetic writing in indigenous and European languages, and they created original paintings that established their own symbolic and iconographic program. When the pictorial wealth and complex meanings of these manuscripts are taken into account, there is a tendency to correlate the painted images with testimonies of "what was written" without considering their materiality and ritual status. Therefore, the intricate, age-old pictorial tradition that includes indigenous codices postdating the Spanish conquest is reduced in modern interpretative practice to viewing these images as mere illustrations: pictorial elucidations, explanations, or amplifications of the written word in a context in which the text—translatable or ready to be reproduced in printed form—is generally equivalent to the civil or ecclesiastical colonizer's authority and control. This interpretational practice restricts the pictorial tradition to the program established by the written text and transforms the images into an apparently redundant expression. Seen in this light, they become minor works executed by the indigenous painter who obeyed the European authority's dictates and epistemology. The painter's creative and intellectual activity is limited to basic imitation (or distortion) of the book engravings or visual repertoires of Italian and Flemish artists, in absolute discontinuity with indigenous pre-Columbian pictography, which is projected as an "authentic," but unattainable and eradicated, cultural horizon.

Diana Magaloni Kerpel's study of the images from the principal document on sixteenth-century Nahua culture, the *Historia general de las cosas de Nueva España* (*General History of the Things of New Spain*), also known as the *Florentine Codex,* operates in a radically different manner. Exploring the materiality, authorship, production, and conceptual and ritual status of the images in the codex, Magaloni Kerpel endeavors to reinstate step-by-step the agency of the *tlacuilos* (indigenous painters) who, in the midst of the cultural destruction and demographic catastrophe of the conquest and colonization, opted to collaborate with Bernardino de Sahagún to ensure the survival of the memory of their society and negotiate the transfer of indigenous knowledge. By combining the scientific arsenal of research on the material nature of the document with the detailed observation of the decisions made by the artists at various moments in the creation of the *Florentine Codex,* Magaloni Kerpel restitutes the complexity of the indigenous painters' work, carried out as they battled to elude the extermination of their civilization by the Europeans and create a fertile path for their own artistic, epistemological, and historical tradition. The *tlacuilos,* Magaloni Kerpel observes, engaged in a dialogue through their images with the texts and paintings of major European artists and authors. The process of creation did not imply mere submission to the dictates of colonial authority.

Instead, the *tlacuilos* embarked upon a true intellectual adventure in which they were active creators who introduced new artistic and intellectual precepts from European books into their own tradition.

This study of the images in the *Florentine Codex* is not simply a display of erudition and methodology. It proposes a radical change in focus regarding the nature of indigenous historical documents akin to that of Sahagún's, which in fact posits the first transaction in cultural anthropology between indigenous and Western peoples in the Americas.

The intellectual and politically bolder hypothesis of Magaloni Kerpel's study suggests that some of the paintings in the *Florentine Codex* are living examples of the indigenous conception of *ixiptlah:* entities activated precisely because they were made as subjects of power, and not as inert objects. Seen from this new optic, the images express themselves in a way distinct from those in Western notions of representation. The author shows that the images were recreated as active subjects through the attire, wrapping, or skin of the pigment and that they assumed their own point of view by possessing a face and a gaze. If Magaloni Kerpel's hypothesis is on the mark, the images in the *Florentine Codex* and in other indigenous documents that were apparently created according to European drawing conventions would be vehicles of a production and expression framed in a native, dissident, and clandestine epistemology. They would appear to be early examples of the resistance struggles of Amerindian epistemology to negotiate the colonizer's communicational and conceptual rules and open a path to the future. Thus, the images would be no longer testimonies on the death of a culture but rather tools of infiltration and continuity. From the codex's pages, we can see the gaze, launched to readers over the centuries, of these beings who had (and who were constituted by) a "point of view."

Cuauhtémoc Medina

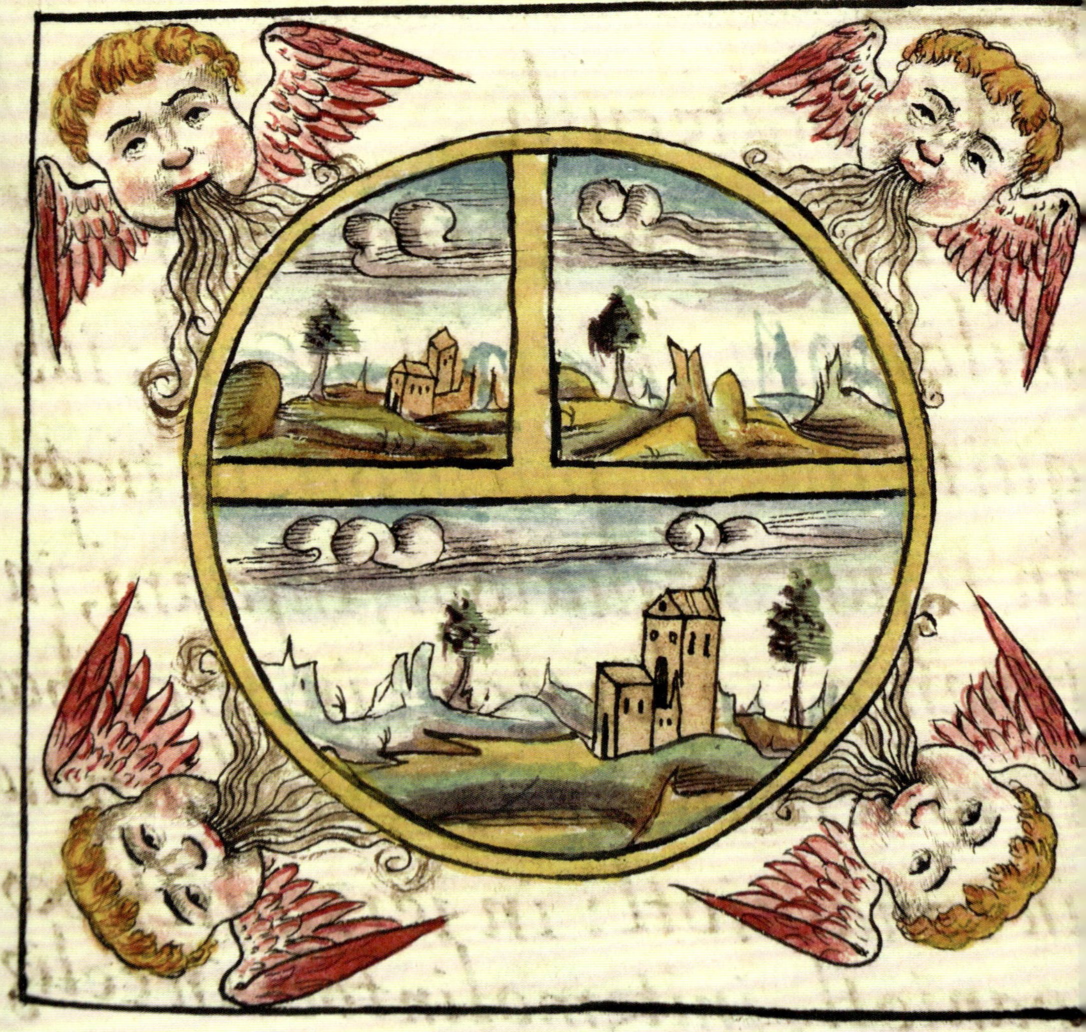

THE COLORS OF THE NEW WORLD

Artists, Materials, and the Creation of the Florentine Codex

Diana Magaloni Kerpel

PART 1
AN INCREDIBLE STORY

The *Historia general de las cosas de Nueva España* (*General History of the Things of New Spain*), also called the *Florentine Codex* (*Códice Florentino*) (ca. 1575–77), is a twelve-volume encyclopedic work written in Nahuatl and Spanish.[1] Today the twelve books are bound together in three copious volumes held at the Laurentian Library in the city of Florence. These illustrated volumes are known collectively as the *Florentine Codex* in honor of the city that houses them. Strictly speaking, the *Historia general de las cosas de Nueva España* refers to the text in Spanish, translated and interpreted by Franciscan friar Bernardino de Sahagún from the original in Nahuatl.[2]

The codex examines the daily life, beliefs, institutions, natural world, and history of the Nahuas, indigenous inhabitants of Central Mexico in the sixteenth century, and their ancestors, the Mexicas.[3] It is the product of an unparalleled historic moment: the conquest of one of the great indigenous civilizations of ancient Mexico by the Spaniards and the creation of a new society and culture that arose from the conflict and dialogue between the native people and the European invaders. Moreover, the codex was physically made during the 1576 epidemic that brutally decimated the indigenous population of Central Mexico, a fact that confers its production with special status akin to a battle waged and won by its creators against extermination and death.

Sahagún brought the *Historia general* to fruition with a group of writers and painters of Nahua origin who have remained anonymous, but this magnum opus would never have come into existence without their active participation. In the prologue to book 2 Sahagún mentions four principal coauthors, whom he refers to as "grammarians" for their ability to read and write Latin, Spanish, and Nahuatl: Antonio Valeriano of Azcapotzalco, Alonso Vegerano of Cuauhtitlan, Martín Jacobita of Tlatelolco, and Pedro de San Buenaventura of Cuauhtitlan. All of them were distinguished indigenous scholars, erudite in their own historical and intellectual tradition as well as that of the seven liberal arts of classical antiquity. Sahagún also provides the names of the scribes who copied the texts: Diego de Grado and Bonifacio Maximiliano, residents of Tlatelolco; and Mateo Severino of Xochimilco.[4] However, many more individuals contributed than were acknowledged by Sahagún; as discussed in this book, at least twenty-two native painters participated in the creation of the *Florentine Codex*. They were expert in the ancient tradition of recording knowledge through paintings, called *tlacuilolli* in Nahuatl, and were trained in the iconography and painting of the European Renaissance style.

The four grammarians, the scribes, and the painters were students or collaborators at the Real Colegio de Santa Cruz Tlatelolco, a school founded in Mexico City in 1536. A veritable humanist project, the school recognized the importance of teaching the indigenous elite about key subjects of European higher learning and Christian theology. It was politically and financially supported by Viceroy Antonio de Mendoza and Bishop Fray Juan de Zumárraga. Renowned members of the Order of Saint Francis, including Sahagún, served as instructors there from 1536. As the years passed and despite its struggles to survive, the Real Colegio de Santa Cruz Tlatelolco became a center for the cultivation of indigenous knowledge, reflection, and culture within the framework of Franciscan teaching. If it were not for the existence of this great institution of higher learning for the indigenous people, the *Florentine Codex* could never have been produced.

The *Florentine Codex* is a complex work of amazing intellectual scope and formidable beauty. In the first place, as noted by historian Ascensión Hernández de León-Portilla, it stands as the first encyclopedic work of a humanist nature created on the American continent that attempts to give the reader almost comprehensive learning through a body of systematized knowledge. It is also the sole work that devotes multiple volumes to documenting specific aspects of Mesoamerican cultures and that approaches the original indigenous voices.[5] In fact, Sahagún's research method included giving questionnaires to individuals of authority in indigenous towns in Central Mexico on aspects of their culture and beliefs. The responses were written in the form of painted documents in consonance with the individuals' own historical traditions; these paintings were then interpreted by the indigenous grammarians and by the painters, who helped shape the texts in Nahuatl recorded in the Latin alphabet[6] and captured in the codex's images.[7]

The twelve sections, referred to as books, contain bilingual texts arranged in two parallel columns: on the right side is the original discussion in Nahuatl, written in the Latin alphabet, while on the left is the Spanish translation. The codex consists of approximately 2,000 pages written and painted by hand and 2,486 magnificent illustrations done in ink and color.[8] The written texts are what most scholars have employed and investigated; indeed, Sahagún's *Historia general* has rightly been regarded as the richest and most important documentary source for understanding the ancient cultures of Mesoamerica. Yet each book also offers a remarkable window on the world of color employed by the Nahuas and their forebears through the insertion of fine ink and color paintings, inscribed in frames in diverse formats and sizes (fig. 1). What I propose to address is the original manuscript as a work of art by studying the process of

FIGURE 1 | OVERLEAF **The *Florentine Codex* open to book 4.** From Bernardino de Sahagún, *Florentine Codex* (ca. 1575–77), bk. 4, fols. 273v–274r. Florence, Biblioteca Medicea Laurenziana.

zeando los vnos, con los otros:
los vnos despreciauan a los o
tros: y cada vno se loaua
asi mjsmo.

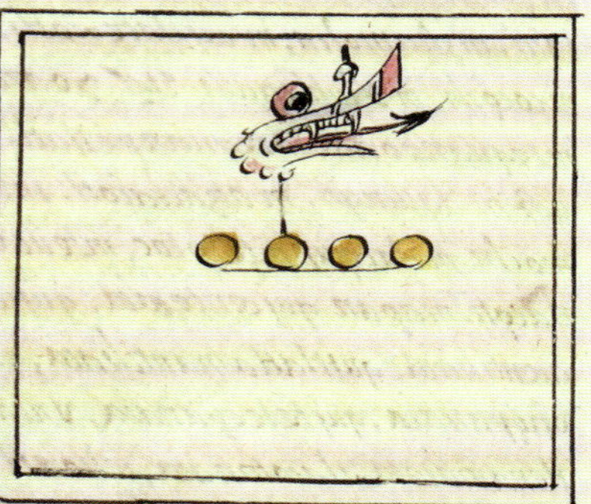

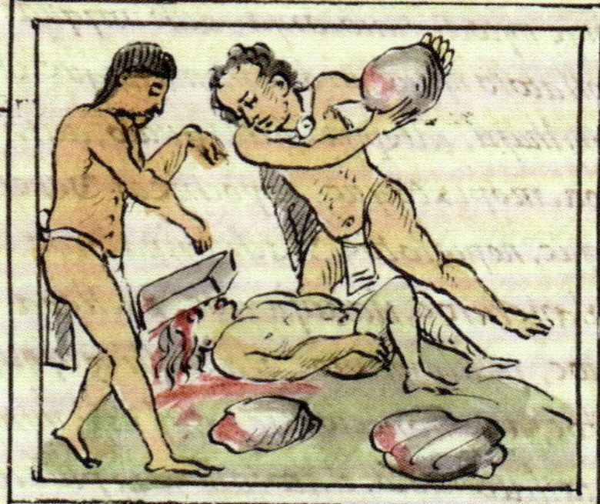

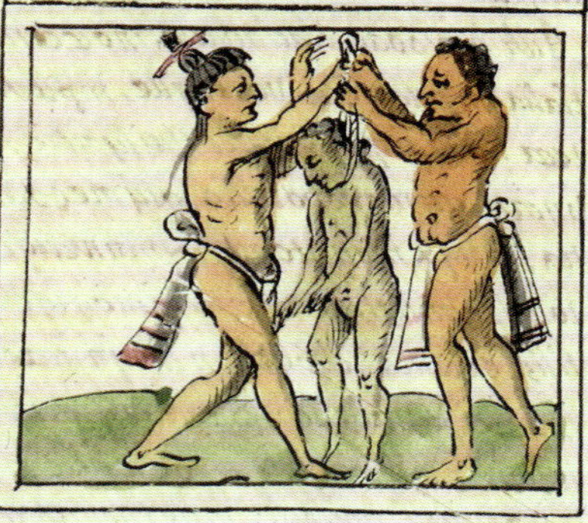

quichiuhtinemj, injc qujlacatzohua
anaoatl, injc ixtlaoatl qujnamje
nemj, injc atlauhtli quitemovitinemj,
noujian calactinemj, in ovica, in a
titlan qujztinemj: auh in nel cana
pan oalmotzaqua, qujnpoloanjchia
cace, vme, inte matitlampaquja,
quj oalcaoa tlatolli, in oalteitoa, i
hoan achtopa qujpetla, quj xitinj
in quauhtenamjtl, quauh tlatzacuj,
ocelotenamjtl, ocelo tlatzacujlli, ic
can qujquequeloa, ica maujltia q
tlatlacaqujta, quj cocoa, qujtotone
quj cocoltuja, quj chichinachilia y
iollo, in acan onmati, in acampa
in acan quentel, in acan icac icx
çannjcam, ine xitlom mooqujchi
çannjcan tianguizco in mjmantin
mj, tlaxtlapalotinemj, çannjcan
motitianquja, tlatlaneujloa, tlat
xiccuj; auh ie vncan mjtoneuhca
pa, motlecomaiavi. vevetzteoa: y
in tlaxcaltiloan, injntlao apaoal
injc vel imjtic oaacic intecoco, int
itic aacic mjtlatol, injntahoan, y
naoan, injc vncan mnecentlalinia
maaoa, mononotza, moquequeloa
mopâpatla, mopapatzaoa, moque
iccatoque, mocoquj motlatoque, mos
tzoujlitoque, moquaquatoque, mj
quáquatoque, motlatol xopeuh toqu
moichoatocatoque, amotenaqujlria
que, amo motenpomaujllanj, chachi

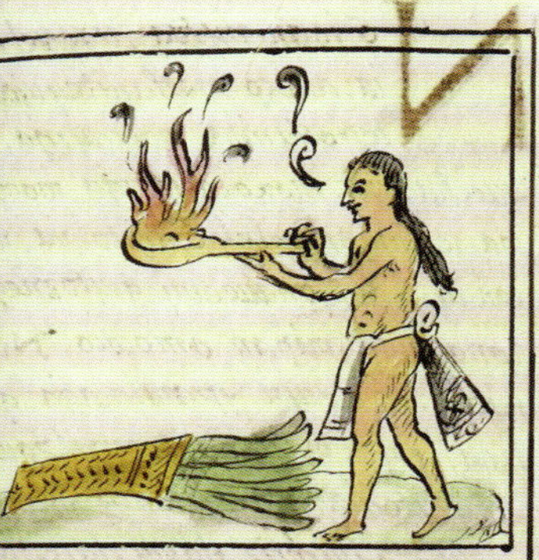

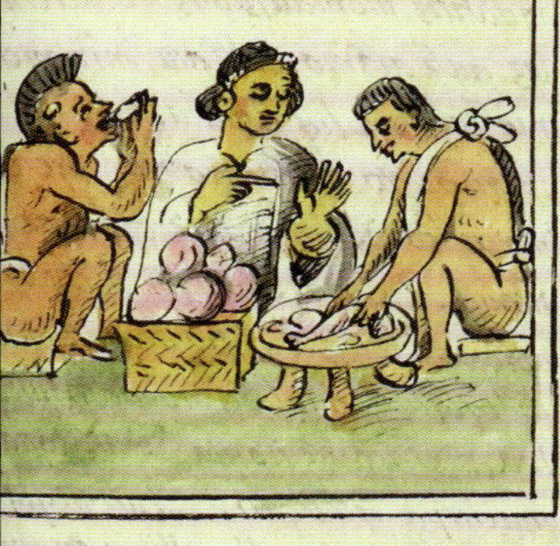

lacatoque, noeac injzmoquixtia: muchitlacatl cecentetl istlatol, atle ipan quimottilitoque, amo com mopouilitoque injnnecujltonol, y njnnetlamachtil: huel nonon qua mutachcauhnequj, mocean tecpoa, cecentecuti, cecenme momati, mocecocamati, nonon qua mottatalhuja: aiac vei in oan tlatoa, aiac vel inpal onmo cencamavia: intlacamo oztome catl, intlacamo vecamatinj: ioan intlacamo cenca mocujttonoa, intlacamo ontlaaaquj ichan, intlacamo tecoanj, intlacamo tealtianj, intlacamo cacatca toc, nananatcatoc ichan cacax tli: intlacamo poctecontica, aio tectica atloa ichan et⁖ Ipam pa injc ceceniaca tlatonaltia ia, puchteca injncacalitic: inj panjn tonalli navecatl.

Capitulo treze, del mal a
[ag]ero que tomauan: si algu
[no] eneste dia tropeçaua, ô se
[l]astimaua en los pies, o caya: y
[de] las malas condiciones delos
[que] nacian, enla octaua ca[sa]
[la] que sellama: chicuey mj
[qui]ztli: donde ay mucho len
[gu]aje de los mal acondicio
[n]ados, hombres, o mugeres.

Injc matlactli vmey ca pitulo, vncan mjtoa: qujl mach amo qualli inezca catca, inaqujn moteputla mjaia, inanoço vetzia, yni panjn: ioan inamo qualli jnpan muchioaia, inaquj que vncan tlacatia, injpan icchicuetetl calli: ynjtoca chicuey mjqujztli: vncan moteneoa injz qujtlamantli in amo qualli intech ca its manufacture; determining the hands of the painters; identifying the nature of the colors; and relating these data to the historical context of its production. In sum, beyond the valuable thematic content of the manuscript, I will show that, through an in-depth approach to the specialized work of producing the paintings, we can understand never-before-seen aspects of the relationship between the creative processes, the nature of the materials used, and the content of the images and texts, which will allow us to open the door to the silent history of the Nahuas who created the paintings together with Sahagún.

In conjunction with a multidisciplinary research project in 2006, I conducted a detailed study of the twelve books that compose the *Florentine Codex.* Together with a research team of chemists headed by Dr. Piero Baglioni from the Università di Firenze, I studied the materials used to write and paint the twelve books and identified the hands of the artist participants and the characteristics that went into the process of the codex's manufacture. The results were always interpreted within their historical context, which raised important questions regarding the underlying rules governing the making of images; the age-old indigenous practice of making painted sacred books; and, obviously, the status and social position of indigenous painters in the sixteenth century. In the sections that follow, I present these reflections in light of the evidence obtained from the scientific and art-historical studies of the codex.[9]

THE TWELVE BOOKS OF THE *FLORENTINE CODEX*

The *Florentine Codex* consists of three bound tomes, cataloged as Mediceo Palatino 218, 219, and 220 by the Laurentian Library. Recent research has revealed evidence that these three volumes were bound in plateresque-style leather covers around 1580, when Sahagún's work was taken to Spain under the care of Fray Rodrigo de Sequera.[10] The history of its journey to Florence remained speculative until art historian Lia Markey found a document dated 1587 by Cardinal Ferdinando de' Medici's librarian that mentions a three-volume work on noteworthy things of New Spain. We know that Cardinal Medici was an avid collector of things from the Americas and that he had the first volume—books 1 to 5—translated into Italian. Upon the death of his brother, Grand Duke Francesco de' Medici, in 1587, the cardinal left the church hierarchy in Rome to occupy the position of Grand Duke of Florence and brought the *Florentine Codex* with him.

As noted, the first volume, Mediceo Palatino 218, contains books 1 to 5, which examine the divine realm and diverse aspects of the ancient religion such as fiestas, ceremonies, the ritual calendar, and auguries. The second volume, Mediceo Palatino 219, covers books 6 to 9, which focus on human aspects such as moral philosophy and rhetoric; astrology; the history of ruling lineages in Central Mexico; and merchants and the craftsmen who specialize in working feathers, precious stones, and metal. The last volume, Mediceo Palatino 220, comprises books 10 to 12, which discuss social customs and natural history as well as the conquest of Mexico.[11]

IMAGES AND TEXTS BETWEEN TWO WORLDS

The relationship between the written sections and the number of illustrations can be understood through Sahagún's point of view, presented in the prologue for each book. There are subjects that he regarded as risky for their idolatrous content but that he justified on the basis of his mission to convert indigenous souls. For example, book 2, which describes ceremonies and human sacrifices, does not have as many images as the text would have needed; on 145 folios there are only 64 illustrations (20 percent). In the same spirit, book 5, devoted to popular beliefs in omens, has only 12 paintings. Topics that were apparently less sensitive—and apparently of less interest as well—such as the artistic procedures of silversmiths and *amanteca* (feather artists), were left untranslated. Book 9, for instance, has a number of folios on which the column usually reserved for the Spanish is instead occupied by a series of framed images (fig. 2). The subject that Sahagún handles with the greatest freedom and at greatest length is natural history in book 11. Clearly the content was in no way threatening, and it was of great interest to the Nahuas and to Sahagún; therefore, it has the largest number of folios (a total of 253) and paintings (965).[12] Another example is book 6, which deals with rhetoric and Nahua moral philosophy; this volume was the

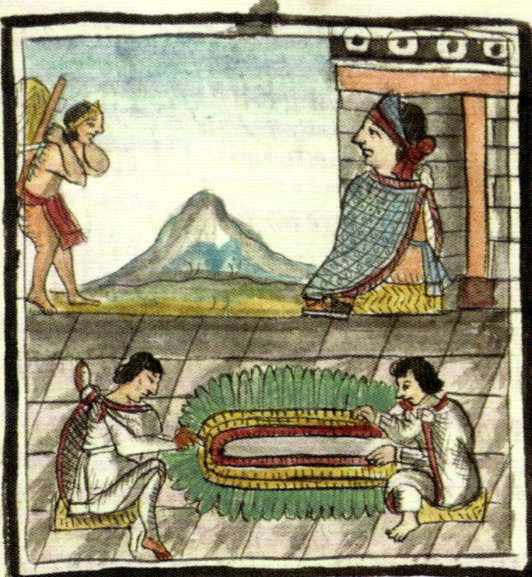

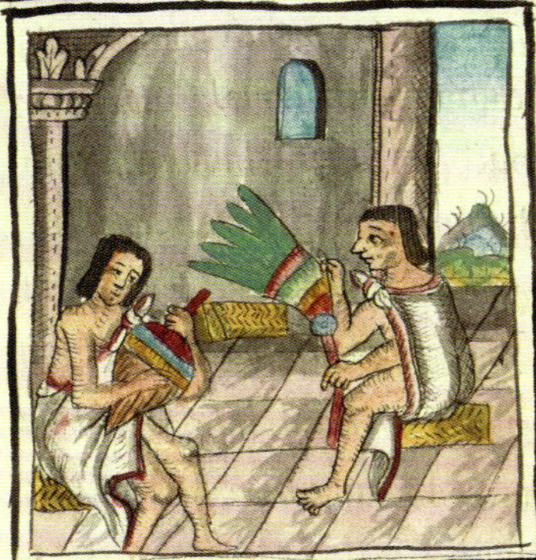

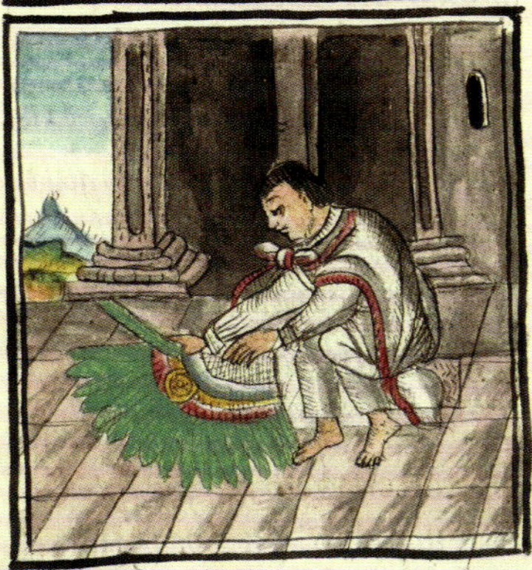

mochi tlaço ihuitl vel ipan tlapiuis:
ic nonqua quintecac, quincaltin cen
tetl calli quinmacac iniscoian inama
tecahoan catca imitech pouia: nepanis
toca in tenochtitlan amanteca ioan
in tlatilulco amanteca. Auh miehoan
tiny, çan quiscahuiaia in quichioaia
itlatqui vitzilobuchtli in quitoca
iotiaia teuquemitl, quetzalquemitl
uitzitzil quemitl, xiuhtotoquemitl,
ic tlatlacuilolli, ic tlatlatlamachilli
in iemochi iniz quican icac tlaçoih-
uitl. Yoan quichioaia iniscoian
itlatqui motecucoma: in quinmaca-
ia, in quintlauhtiaia icoahoan in
altepetl ipan tlatoque, ic monotzaia
motenehoaia tecpan amanteca
istul tecahoan in tlacatl. Auh in ce
quintin, motenehoaia calpiscan
amanteca, itech pouia inizquitetl
icaca icalpiscacal motecucoma:
iehoatl quichioaia, intlein imaceh
allatqui motecucoma inipan ma
cehoaia, mitotiaia: inicoac ilhuitl
quiçaia, quitlatlattitia, quitlane
nectiaia, inçaço catlehoatl queleuiz
inipan mitotiz: ca cecentlamantli
iecauia, cecentlamantli quichioaia

most praised by Sahagún, for he dedicated it to Fray Rodrigo de Sequera, his principal supporter in the Franciscan order. All the paintings in book 6 were rendered in tones of gray, white, and black, imitating engravings, which gives it an appearance similar to that of printed books at the time. It is probable that these images were intentionally devoid of color to make them seem as authoritative as those made by artists like Albrecht Dürer (see fig. 8).[13]

Are the paintings in the *Florentine Codex* simple illustrations to support the text? Are they done solely to make the manuscript more beautiful? Why is there a change in the colors and pigments employed in each book? Are these paintings, despite a Europeanizing style distant from the conventions of the indigenous style, as significant as the images from ancient Mexican codices?[14] In the pages that follow, I offer an example that helps clarify the paintings' function as a significant means of communication for the indigenous vision, although this does not seem to have had the same preponderance in Sahagún's mind.

THE PAINTINGS: OBJECTS OR SUBJECTS?

The first six folios of book 1 present the complex of ancient gods in a format unique in the *Florentine Codex*. Each folio is divided into four large rectangles, and each rectangle contains the representation of a god. This way of dividing the pages into four is inspired by formats employed in Mesoamerican painted books, such as the folios dedicated to the twenty deities and the eighty days in the *Codex Borgia*.[15] In book 1 of the *Florentine Codex*, however, the alphabetic writing serves to connect the images to the written texts: each god bears his or her name in Nahuatl and a reference to the chapter in which all the information on that deity is described in writing. Paynal, the representative of Huitzilopochtli (the Aztec patron god), appears in the lower left quadrant of the first folio of book 1. The detail shows a figure—richly attired with a cape and feather headdress—who is seated and in profile (fig. 3). The text in Spanish states that Paynal is "Huitzilopochtli's *vicario* [substitute]," the *capitán mayor* (military leader), who set out light-footed and swift to face enemies in war. It also tells of the fiesta during which priests wore Paynal costumes and ran quickly throughout the city in a procession. The text explains that this is the way the priests personified the swiftness required by warriors when they clashed with the enemy.[16] The static image of the figure does not correspond to the actions described in the text; the figure serves the reader simply as a reference point.

In contrast, the narrative in the parallel column in Nahuatl is closely related to the painting. It mentions that Paynal is a *moteixiptlatiani*—that is to say, the incarnated image of Huitzilopochtli.[17] This word is derived from the concept of *ixiptlah,* which means "image, substitute of something or someone." Furthermore, the text focuses attention on the image by referring to the attributes of the costume: "And he [Paynal] was thus arrayed: he went garbed in the costly cape of precious feathers. The quetzal feather device went placed on him. He had bars painted upon his face; he had the star design painted upon his face. . . . He had a turquoise nose rod. His was the hummingbird disguise. He had the breast mirror; he had a shield set with a mosaic of turquoise."[18]

It should be noted that the representation is very close to the description in Nahuatl; in fact, the round shield has an asymmetrical design that indicates a "mosaic of turquoise" and the figure's face displays horizontal bands along with small circles around the eyes that are the sign for "star." Here it is worth taking a moment to explore the crucial relationship between the proximity of the detailed descriptions of the costume in the Nahuatl text, the painted figure, and the comment that Paynal is the *ixiptlah* of Huitzilopochtli.

The Nahuatl word *ixiptlah,* or *teixiptlah,* represents a complex concept that refers to objects and people, both of which can serve as representatives of or substitutes for someone, even a god. According to Alfredo López Austin's explanation of the concept, the key is the morpheme *xip,* which is derived from the verb *xipehua,* "to flay," "to peel the skin." The concept of *ixiptlah* can thus be related to the notion of *nahualli,* which

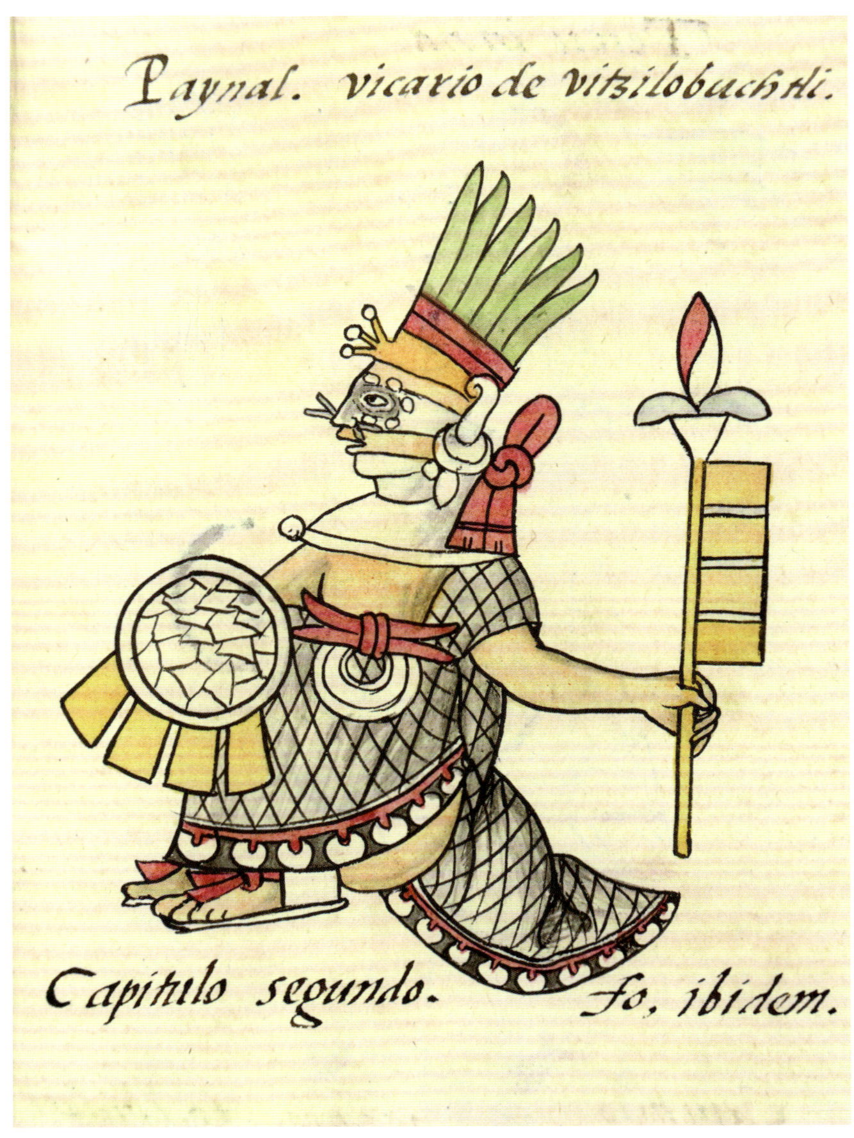

FIGURE 3 | *Paynal, vicario de vitsilobuchtli* (Paynal, Huitzilopochtli's substitute). From Bernardino de Sahagún, *Florentine Codex* (ca. 1575–77), bk. 1, fol. 10r (detail). Florence, Biblioteca Medicea Laurenziana.

López Austin states is the capacity of a powerful individual to transform himself into another being and adopt the other's identity. The wearer is described as possessing "the vestments of the other," his "skin" or "covering," and thus having been transformed.[19] The *ixiptlah* receives the hot, luminous force of the numen and adopts his identity by donning his "skin or covering." This luminous force, the author tells us, could also be projected on objects and representations, which at times were charged with so much energy that no one could look at them directly.[20] Salvador Reyes Equiguas, complementing López Austin's ideas, posits that the *ixiptlah* were always the product of human creation: sculptures in stone, wood, edible dough, or else a live slave wearing a costume. They could also be paintings on paper, hide, or stucco.[21] Reyes Equiguas points out that the word *ixiptlah* has the morpheme *ix[tli]* as well, where *ixtli* is "face," "eye."[22] These two words that possibly compose *ixiptlah* are significant. As mentioned above, *ixtli*, "eye," also means "face," while the verb *xipehua*, "to flay," is associated with the flayed skin of animals or war captives worn by warriors, priests, and kings as a symbol of having acquired more power and multiple identities.[23] The complexity of this concept, between representation and presence with its own point of view, can be applied to the images in the *Florentine Codex*.

The very text in Nahuatl tells us: Paynal is the *ixiptlah* of Huitzilopochtli. This statement was accepted by Nahua painters and writers, who acted in accord with a principle that was obvious to them as they defined Paynal through the component parts of his attire, his "covering." However, these facts are not easily apprehended by twenty-first-century Western readers, nor were they clear to Sahagún. The symbolic and cognitive operation of the Nahuatl text and of the painted image is to make Paynal's *ixiptlah* "appear," not merely to have it be the illustration or ornamentation of information on the ancient gods.[24] Thus, to the Nahuas, the action of painting and the painting itself responded to different rules than those we are familiar with today.

These differences may be understood if we recall that Nahuas, like other Amerindian cultures, lived in a universe in which the stars, water, mountains, and some objects were regarded as beings that were as animated and alive as animals and people. In his pioneering ethnographic work, Eduardo Viveiros de Castro concludes that, in Amerindian ontologies, "all beings that are attributed a point of view will be a subject"; in other words, "whoever is activated or set in action by a point of view will be a subject."[25] Furthermore, Viveiros de Castro indicates that, because everything in nature shares a spirit that imbues it with life, the difference between beings is expressed and defined by using the body and attire. That is to say, the concept of "covering" is as essential as that of "point of view," because it is the exterior form that defines a subject: "it is not so much that the body is a sort of clothing but that the attire is a type of body."[26] From this perspective, some paintings could be understood as *ixiptlah*—a covering with a specific form, illuminated with colors, something that possesses eyes and therefore a point of view—and thus be regarded as activated subjects, not objects, as we have conceived of them in the West.

The text in Spanish shows the other reality of the images in the *Florentine Codex*. In the prologue to book I, Sahagún clearly states his objectives. He explains why he wants his volume illustrated, despite the fact that the paintings represented a considerable investment of work that in some way contravened the Franciscan vow of poverty.[27] First, Sahagún declares that his work will help in the true conversion of the indigenous people, because idolatry is a disease of the soul and good doctors of souls, such as missionaries, have to know the symptoms if they are to remedy the ailment. He goes on to mention his goal of having all the words and metaphors recorded in Nahuatl. However, Sahagún also notes that to achieve these goals, a work of the breadth and scope of his *Historia general* is actually not necessary; a work so beautifully produced is meant to spread awareness of "the degree of perfection of this Mexican people, which has not yet been known, because there came over them that curse which Jeremiah . . . thundered upon Judea and Jerusalem."[28] Ultimately, the work attests to the true value of the Nahuas in the context of the apocalyptic devastation they had suffered. This idea is key to understanding the *Florentine Codex* in its function as a bicultural and multiauthored work, because it is at this point, as will be demonstrated in the following sections, that the intent of the indigenous people and the Franciscan friar coalesced.

In 1576, as the team in Tlatelolco was immersed in working on the *Florentine Codex,* a devastating epidemic struck Central Mexico. The epidemic targeted the indigenous population, which was drastically reduced as a result.[29] The widespread outbreak was so serious that even Sahagún, in book 11, felt compelled to interrupt his Spanish translation and switch to first person to bear witness to what was happening around him:

> Now, in this year of 1576, in the month of August a general and great plague began, which already continues for three months. Many people have died, die, and every day more are dying. . . . I am now in this city of Mexico, in the district of Tlatilulco [Tlatelolco], and I see that from the time it began until today, the 8th of November, the number of dead has always gone increasing: from ten [to] twenty, from thirty to forty, from fifty to sixty and to eighty. And from here on I do not know what will be. In this plague [1576], as well as the one mentioned above [1545], many died of hunger and from not having anyone to cure them nor provide what was necessary. It happened and happens in many homes, that all those of the house become sick without there being anyone who might offer a pitcher of water.[30]

Other indigenous documents confirm the epidemic's exterminating effect on the indigenous population: "The second plague that there was in New Spain was in this year [1576], which resulted in the final destruction of this land. It lasted more than a year. . . . There was a census of the Indians and it was found that more than two million died."[31] During this time, the group from Santa Cruz Tlatelolco was working on books 11 and 12. Despite the fact that the Nahua painters were at risk of illness and struck by profound sorrow over the utter loss left in the wake of the epidemic, they made a courageous decision: to fight off death and finish the *Florentine Codex* with images of unsurpassed quality. This leads to an essential question: What did the *Florentine Codex* mean to the Tlatelolco team who decided to devote their lives to completing it amid a mortal battle against death itself?

The natural history section in book 11 has outstanding examples revealing not only that the indigenous artists had learned to copy European models from the numerous prints from Europe that were in circulation in the Americas but also that they had gone beyond the mechanical act of copying, by incorporating into their practice pictorial concepts that were being debated by artists during the European Renaissance.[32] As Tom Cummins has proposed, the native painters had, through books and prints, formed a community that participated in a global culture.[33] In fact, by reading indigenous documents from this period, we can see that the Nahuas, without losing their own cultural identity, sought to incorporate themselves into the globalized world that they belonged to after the Spanish conquest. For example, the text known as the *Anales de Juan Bautista* records the practice of a Nahua painters' guild from 1564 to 1569 in Mexico City. According to the *Anales,* the painters were *pillis* (nobles), educated for generations in artistic traditions. They constituted organized, active groups that operated the *tlacuilocalli* (painting workshop), and they employed a wide range of pictorial and sculptural techniques. Furthermore, the text highlights how the painters maintained an ongoing dialogue in their practice with diverse social groups: with their teachers, the priests Pedro de Gante, Bernardino de Sahagún, and Alonso de Molina; with indigenous rulers; and with colonial authorities.[34] Another notorious example of the vast knowledge of the world that the Nahuas possessed at that time is the *Libro de los guardianes y gobernadores de Cuauhtinchan (1519–1640)* (Book of the guardians and rulers of Cuauhtinchan [1519–1640]), which, following an annals format, recorded the important events in the local history of this town. It is noteworthy that events regarded as significant by the historians of a small, remote settlement in the Sierra de Puebla included not only what took place in Cuauhtinchan and other regions of New Spain but also what transpired in faraway lands. For instance, the entry for 1532 records the start of one of the mortal epidemics in New Spain as well as the "start of the heresy in England over the passions and bad example of King Henry VIII." In 1535 and 1536, both the founding in New Spain of a school for the sons of the indigenous nobility and the rebellion in the city of Geneva against the Duke of Savoy were recorded.[35] These examples show that indigenous groups were integrated into global history from their own tradition. Indeed, the pictorial phenomenon of the images in the *Florentine Codex* is also part of this sixteenth-century Nahua intellectual process of extending the object of history to a broader geography and, as I will present in the following sections, a broader temporality.[36]

PAINTING AND KNOWLEDGE: *IN TLILLI IN TLAPALLI*

Figure 4 shows the *coiametl,* a wild pig or peccary from the tropical rain forests of southern Mesoamerica.[37] Remarkably, the painting employs pictorial and graphic resources that were considered avant-garde in Europe in 1576: it has an outline defined by means of a continuous, precise line, as prescribed by the *disegno* (drawing) rules in Renaissance treatises. At the same time, the line uses graphic resources from printed books to delineate details on the face, body, and pelt. One can note a superb handling of *colorire* (coloring) techniques: the gray, with brown nuances, constructs the animal's body with light and shadow. The background landscape shows synthetic brushstrokes of colors juxtaposed to create the illusion of open space. The ground is painted in yellow and red, and the vegetation is green, which fuses with the bright blue of the distant mountains. The sky is left uncolored and in this way the painter was able to include colors as another aspect of the image, thus merging two pictorial forms: painting and engraving.[38] (It is interesting to note that Alonso de Molina translates the Nahuatl word *tlaixiuiliztli* as both "perspective" and "art.")[39] Finally, the painter intelligently plays with the viewer: at the same time that he offers a realistic figure, in solid alignment with the artistic value of *imitatore della natura* (imitation of nature),[40] he transforms the peccary into a simple representation by including the animal in a small rectangle. However, the painter again insists on the ambiguity between reality and invention, having the peccary emerge from the frame that contains it by treading on that frame with its feet, as if imbued with its own vitality. As Michael Baxandall has demonstrated, the pictorial skill shown through an artist's work reflects a society's visual and cognitive culture. Artistic style is, in this sense, a way of perceiving reality, and a painting is in itself the repository of a series of interactions and social

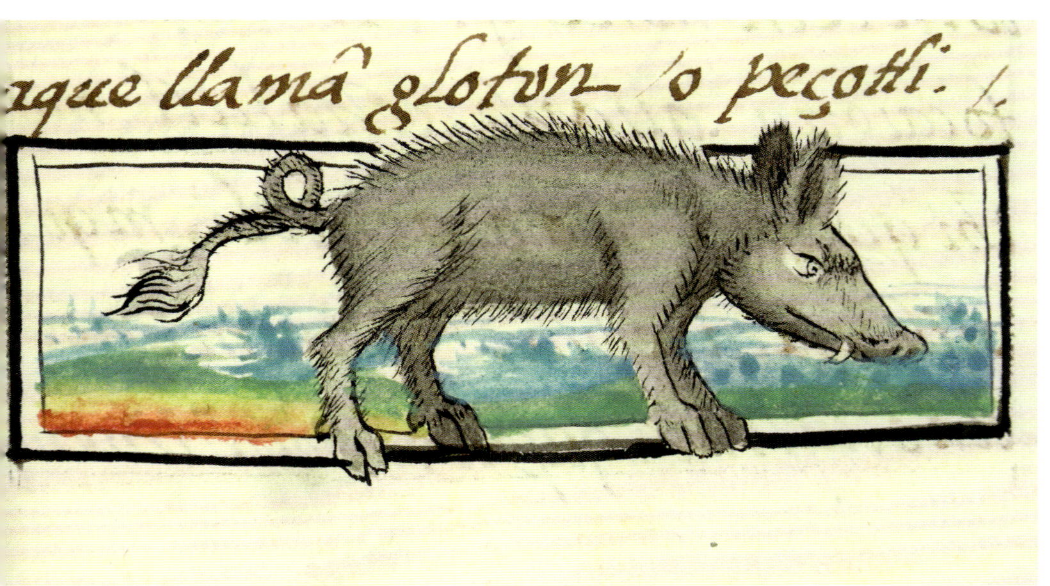

FIGURE 4 | *Coiametl* (peccary). From Bernardino de Sahagún, *Florentine Codex* (ca. 1575–77), bk. 11, fol. 165r (detail). Florence, Biblioteca Medicea Laurenziana.

values.[41] The painter of the peccary in the *Florentine Codex* utilized conventions and skills appreciated by the art world and society of his time, beyond the confines of Tlatelolco; with his art he was projected toward Europe to occupy his position as an indigenous painter from New Spain, in a world in which proving one's worth as an artist was a political action of negotiation to defend social status and freedom.[42]

The *Anales de Juan Bautista* contains an exhortation to painters that warns: "Oh *toltecaye* [artists], none of you heeded the words of your fathers, but investigate your ancestry, your work as artists came precisely from them, enter into the interior of their nobility . . . but remember your commitment, your ordinances."[43] As a matter of fact, the respected artists known as the *toltecaye* were now a generation born in New Spain and therefore could not have heard from their forebears who had died in the conquest. Nonetheless, they belonged to the indigenous tradition—they were its heirs. Displaying visual habits of the vanguard at that time did not imply that the *toltecaye* had dismissed from their practice the fundamental idea of the significant and openly powerful role exerted by images in the Mesoamerican artistic tradition. On the contrary, painting was also a ritual action that made the unknown appear and exist; this idea is present in the representation of Paynal and his status as *ixiptlah* in book 1 (see fig. 3). The perception that the act of painting images was a means of activating them as subjects may also be found in the *Anales de Juan Bautista,* which refers to the production of a silver sculpture of Our Lady the Virgin of Guadalupe as if the sculpture made "her *ixiptlah* appear."[44]

The purpose of the image in the Mesoamerican world corresponded with that of writing in the Western world: to record and build knowledge. However, as we have seen, paintings have an inherently distinct nature because they are conceived as subjects. In Nahuatl the notion of recording history vis-à-vis these subject-paintings is expressed in the metaphor *in tlilli in tlapalli* (the black ink, the colors), which, according to Miguel León-Portilla, was used to refer to the knowledge acquired and accumulated by a culture—its wisdom.[45] The expression reveals something of crucial importance, for it describes wisdom by means of its constituent materials: *in tlilli* (the black ink) alludes to the outline of painted figures, while *in tlapalli* (the colors) refers to the pigments that illuminate them with their brilliant hues.[46] For two millennia Mesoamerica conceived of images in this way. The studies I performed on color and artists in the *Florentine Codex* explore this proposal in greater depth.

PART 2
REPAINTING THE WORLD

THE *TOLTECAYE* AND THE NAHUA TREATISE ON PAINTING

Book II of the *Florentine Codex* devotes chapter II to the procedures for "making all the colors."[47] Despite the chapter's brevity, one can say that it represents a veritable Nahua treatise on the art of painting, so I will continue to refer to it in this way. Following the Renaissance tradition, the Nahua treatise is inspired by the work of Pliny the Elder and his *Naturalis historia* (*Natural History*). In fact, it has been proposed that Pliny's encyclopedia was one of the models followed in the preparation of the *Florentine Codex,* and we know that a copy of *Naturalis historia* existed in the Real Colegio de Santa Cruz Tlatelolco library.[48] Moreover, as Serge Gruzinski has noted, the Renaissance model of regarding classical antiquity as the source of knowledge and inspiration served to build a vision that established a parallel between the American past and the civilizations of ancient Greece and Rome. In this sense, Pliny was employed as a guide to writing the natural history of the New World; for instance, Francisco Hernández's *Historia natural de Nueva España* (Natural history of New Spain) was written with the participation of indigenous physicians from Santa Cruz Tlatelolco.[49] However, based on the way the information in the Nahua treatise is presented, it is clear that the painters were also familiar with the discourse surrounding painting based on the work of Pliny the Elder; in the Nahua treatise the parallelism between the classical past and pictorial practice itself is presented through the portraits of the artists who painted the *Florentine Codex,* making the *toltecaye* true artists in the tradition of Apelles.[50]

Pliny organized his *Naturalis historia* into thirty-seven books with independent subjects that encompass all spheres of knowledge. Books 33, 34, and 35 were fundamental works during the Renaissance for exploring the capacity and role of the pictorial and sculptural arts. In these sections Pliny discusses metals, minerals, and pigments. Despite the fact that his taxonomy is based on Aristotle and Theophrastus, Pliny does not follow their metallurgical classification. Instead, he classifies these materials in accordance with their uses in art, thus establishing a direct relationship between the raw material as part of nature and the artist's capacity to understand it and transform it. For Pliny it is this capacity to transform and recreate nature that grants the artist the intellectual status of *artifex* (craftsman, maker) and *inventore* (creator). During the Renaissance, these ideas made it possible to discuss the status of painting as a liberal art, not only a mechanical one (as it had been deemed in the Middle Ages).[51]

This central idea—of painting being a liberal art—seems to have been applied by the artists of the *Florentine Codex*. Book 11 imitates the structure of *Naturalis historia:* Pliny's books 33, 34, and 35 deal with metals, stones, and minerals according to their uses in sculpture and painting, and chapters 9, 10, and 11 in book 11 discuss metal and stone as material for sculpture, as well as the colors used in painting. The parallel is not merely formal—it has a deeper significance.

In book 35 Pliny examines the poetic capacity of painting to imitate nature and recreate it using ingenuity; in this sense, he expresses his esteem for ancient Greek artists: "Although Apelles, Aition, Melanthius and Nicomachus, all illustrious painters, only used four colours, . . . their works were sold individually for more than the total worth of an entire city . . . there is no longer noble painting . . . now we only appreciate the richness of the material and not that of the mind."[52] Pliny describes the materials used as pigments in their natural state and cites their compositions, while he expresses his opinion on the quality of colors that they produce. At the end of the chapter he lists the names of great artists of ancient Greece, including Apelles.[53]

The Nahua treatise follows Pliny's concepts and adapts them to the tradition of the *toltecaye,* employing two different resources—writing and painting—to describe "all the colors," how they were obtained from nature, the way they were produced, and how people painted with them. The treatise also provides a list of the *toltecaye*. In fact, the painters and writers of the Nahua treatise follow Pliny's reasoning by relating the natural state of the materials in their environment to knowledge of nature, and then relating that knowledge to the transformative capacity of the *artifex* and the creativity of the *inventore*. However, the *toltecaye,* unlike Pliny, regard the raw materials as part of the covering that imbues identity to the image; indeed, these raw materials, as we have seen, play a fundamental role in defining and activating the image as the subject, or *ixiptlah*.[54]

The Nahua treatise organizes information according to a system of complementary polarities. The colors are divided into those obtained from plants and insects and those found as minerals in the earth. Saturated, vibrant, and light colors are contrasted with those that are dilute, opaque, and dark.[55] There is also a distinction between primary colors (red, blue, yellow, black, and white) and secondary hues (green, purple, brown, and ochre), which are obtained by mixing. Inks used for writing are discussed separately.

The first color mentioned in the Nahua treatise is the red (*nochez-tli*) obtained from the cochineal insect. The Spanish text states that this valuable color was exported to "China and Turkey and almost all over the world."[56] In the corresponding Nahuatl text the origin of the color's name is explained: it derives from the words *nochtli* (prickly pear) and *eztli* (blood) because cochineal is formed on prickly pear pads and resembles blood. Cochineal, it tells us, is a worm, and the prickly pear is the place where it is born and grows.[57] The image illustrating these passages is divided into two sections and provides additional information on the pictorial techniques. The upper section depicts the prickly pear in its natural setting with insects on its pads and some of them oozing a red dye onto the ground (fig. 5). This image, following Pliny, represents the raw material in its natural state. The lower section divides the pictorial space into two locations and times: on the left is the maker of the color (*artifex*) and on the right is the painter (*inventore*), who is seen at work inside a building in New Spain, possibly a sixteenth-century *tlacuilocalli* (painting workshop).

The texts and particular manner of the images reveal the elements that constitute the pictorial practice of the *toltecaye*. Figure 6 depicts another way of making colors: blending, which is one form of ingenuity praised by Pliny. It shows the production of the color green known as *quiltic* (tender grass, Maya green), used to paint quetzal feathers, which were highly prized in Mesoamerican visual arts (fig. 7; see fig. 2).

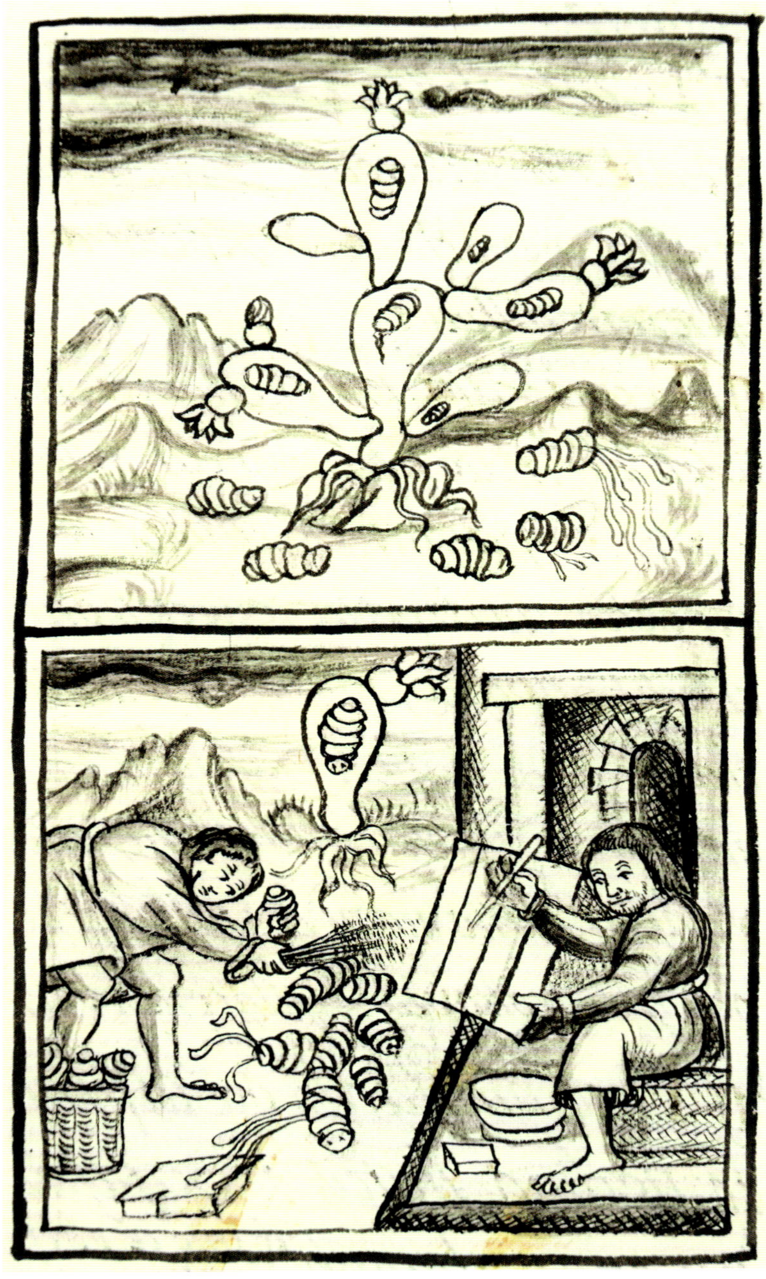

FIGURE 5 | **The process of obtaining and producing *nocheztli* (cochineal).** From Bernardino de Sahagún, *Florentine Codex* (ca. 1575–77), bk. 11, fol. 368v (detail). Florence, Biblioteca Medicea Laurenziana.

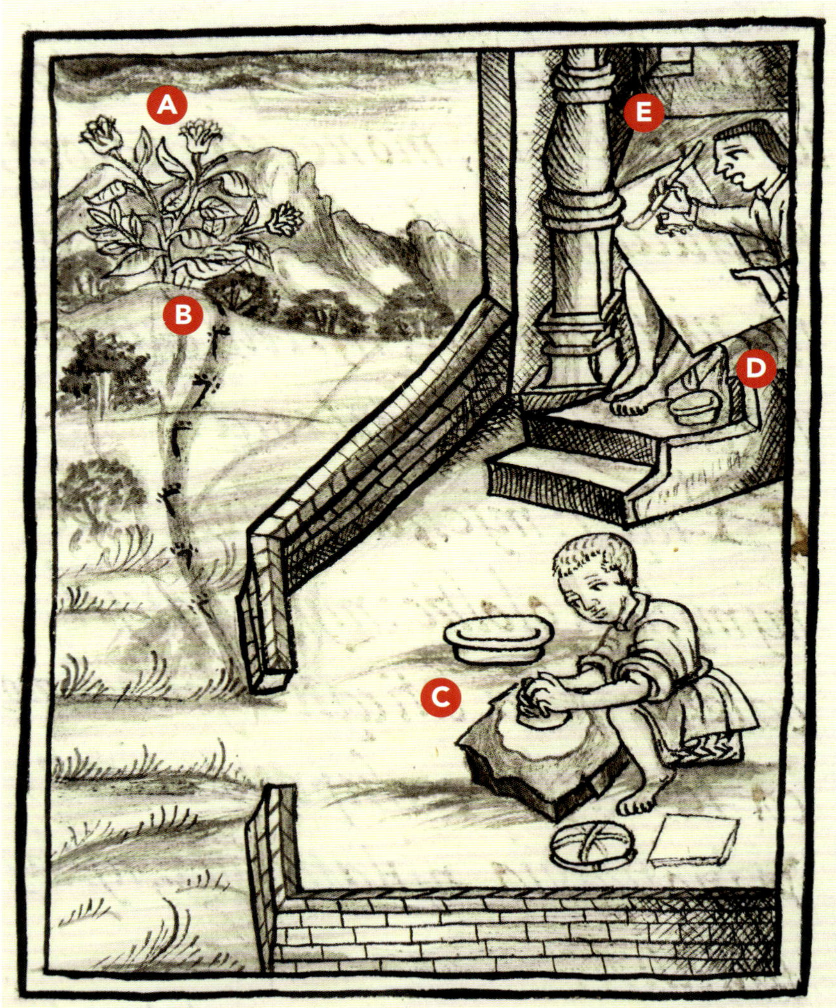

FIGURE 6 | The production of *quiltic* (Maya green). A. Raw material; B. Source of the indigo; C. Process used to make *quiltic*; D. The *tlacuilo* (painter) and his tools; and E. The place where the *tlacuilo* paints. From Bernardino de Sahagún, *Florentine Codex* (ca. 1575–77), bk. 11, fol. 372v (detail). Florence, Biblioteca Medicea Laurenziana.

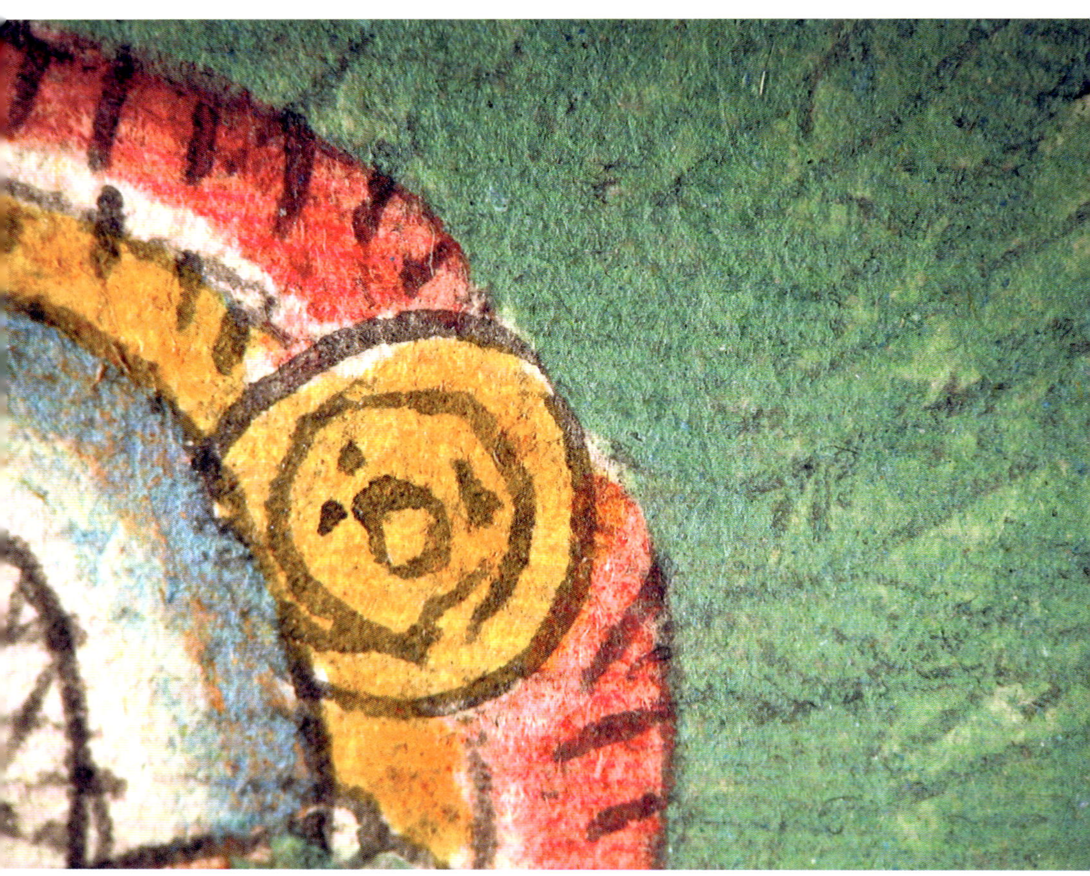

FIGURE 7 | Detail of the quetzal feathers in headdress, photograph
of the original seen through a stereomicroscope at
magnification x10 (see fig. 2). From Bernardino de
Sahagún, *Florentine Codex* (ca. 1575–77), bk. 9, fol. 370r
(detail). Florence, Biblioteca Medicea Laurenziana.

The texts explain that painters had to mix light blue *texotli* (Maya blue) with yellow *zacatlaxcalli* and agglutinate them with *tzacutli,* a gum extracted from orchid pseudobulbs.[58] The painting that illustrates the production of *quiltic* expands the information (see fig. 6), and we can identify

A. The raw material. In this case, it is the indigo plant that produces blue.
B. The source of the indigo. The image shows a long path leading to a distant spot, representing the tropical region in which indigo plants grow.
C. The process used to make *quiltic*. An assistant grinds the two colors on a smooth stone. The disk with a cross is the "yellow tortilla" *zacatlaxcalli,* and the *texotli* is a rectangular bar. Also visible is a receptacle in which to mix the blue and yellow and then dilute them in water and *tzacutli* to prepare the green paint.
D. The *tlacuilo* (painter) and his tools. The artist will paint on a sheet of cloth using the dissolved green color and a brush.
E. The place where the *tlacuilo* paints.

Each illustration constitutes a text on the *toltecaye*'s painting art, set in the present of New Spain (see figs. 5, 6). Moreover, upon closer examination, we can see how the painters and their helpers are rendered as individuals: each one has a distinctive face, a particular way of arranging his hair, and specific attire. Twenty paintings show the production of one color or another in the Nahua treatise; in all of them the depictions of the painters are portraits. It is possible that, following Pliny the Elder, the authors of the Nahua treatise on painting provide through their portraits the list of the great *toltecaye* who executed the *Florentine Codex.* This means of representation—which includes the portrait of the text's author, generally shown painting or writing in his workshop—continues a long tradition of illuminated manuscripts from the time of the Middle Ages.[59] I suggest that the artists are showing themselves to the reader just as Pliny presented the followers of Apelles: they are the *toltecaye* of New Spain, heirs to the great tradition *in tlilli in tlapalli* (fig. 8).

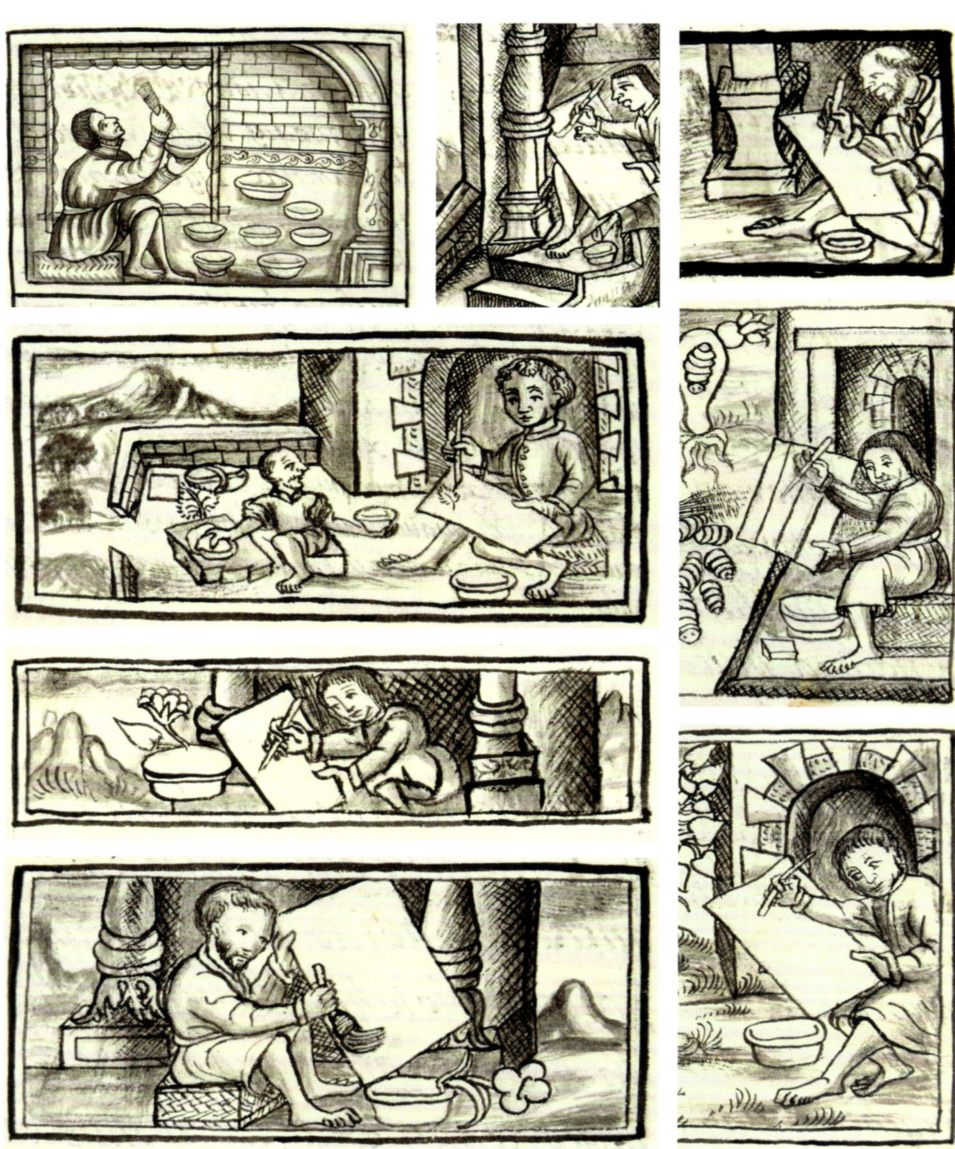

FIGURE 8 | **Portraits of several painters.** From Bernardino de Sahagún, *Florentine Codex* (ca. 1575–77), details from bk. 11. Clockwise from top left: fols. 373v, 372v, 371r, 368v, 369v, 369v, 369r, 372v. Florence, Biblioteca Medicea Laurenziana.

How can we determine how many artists participated in the creation of the *Florentine Codex?* Sahagún left the names of only four main grammarians (named as coauthors at the beginning of this book) and three of the scribes who wrote the texts.[60] The great work, however, was the result of a truly collective effort in which a group of Nahua grammarians, painters, and writers, together with Sahagún, came face-to-face with death—the 1576 epidemic—like brave warriors, armed with quill pens, brushes, paper, and colors.

One can approach these anonymous painters through their depictions of themselves working as artists (see fig. 8).[61] Therefore, it is possible to identify twenty-two painters on the basis of how the eyes, the profile of the nose and chin, and the proportions of parts of the body have been drawn.[62] It is also possible to distinguish between different artists' treatment of line—that is to say, the force of the line, its mobility and precision, and the graphic resources employed to give volume to the figures. There was clearly a principal painter, whom I will refer to as the Master of Both Traditions, and three other master painters who produced images of greater narrative complexity and possessed a more refined quality of execution.

The Master of the Three-Quarter Profiles can be recognized by the scale of his human figures, which are diminutive in proportion and generally shown in three-quarter view (fig. 9). The Master of Long Noses painted many of the images in books 6 and 10, which illustrate moral philosophy and social customs, subjects that were introduced into sixteenth-century pictorial practice. The Master of Complex Skin Coloring is identified by his lines, recalling drawings and engravings from the Italian Renaissance; and by the skin tones of his figures, revealing his knowledge of the European oil-painting tradition in which various pigments were combined to achieve a flesh tone (fig. 10).

The most important painter, the Master of Both Traditions, painted all of book 7 and many of the images in books 3, 8, 11, and 12. He was a master of drawing and color, but what should be highlighted is his creation of a new style, in which he deploys pictorial skill and visual habits from both pre-Hispanic and Renaissance traditions. His paintings purposefully

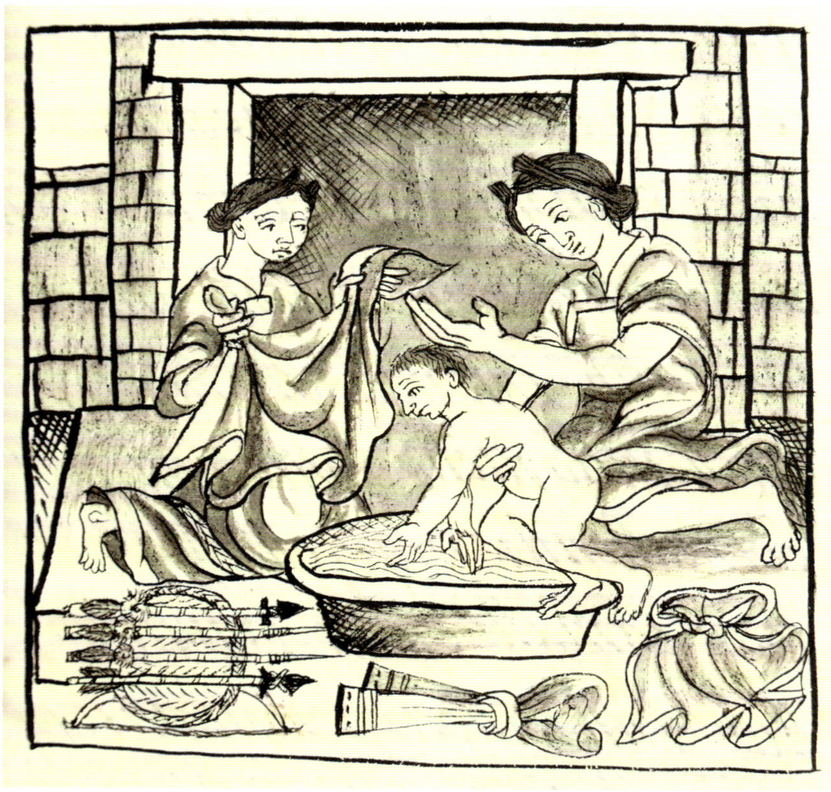

FIGURE 9 | **Master of the Three-Quarter Profiles.** Midwife. From Bernardino de Sahagún, *Florentine Codex* (ca. 1575–77), bk. 6, fol. 174r (detail). Florence, Biblioteca Medicea Laurenziana.

evoke times and contexts from the indigenous past and from the present of New Spain. Figure 11 shows the Master of Both Traditions' depiction of Cuauhtemoc, the last *tlatoani,* or Aztec ruler, from book 8. The principal master employs the formal conventions of the ancient indigenous pictorial tradition: Cuauhtemoc as the ruler wears the *xiuhuitzolli* (royal blue diadem); his name is recorded in the form of a glyph, "descending eagle"; he is positioned in profile on his *in petlatl, in icpalli* (royal woven mat seat), which conveys his authority and dignity; and he is shown covered with a fine cotton cape, a prestigious indication of power.[63]

In another painting, from book 7, the Master of Both Traditions has devised a new way of representing the sun and the solar phenomenon of an

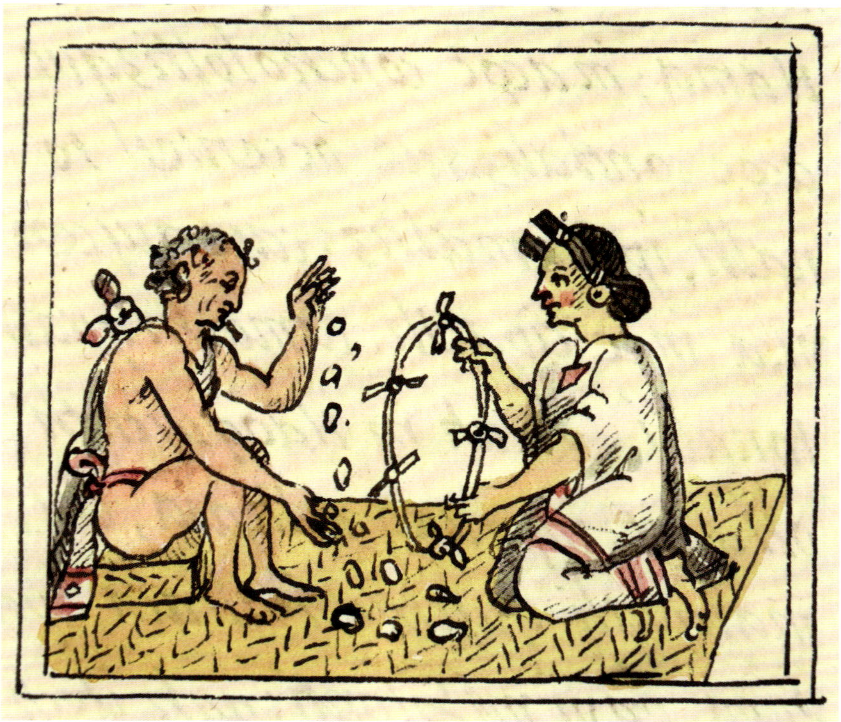

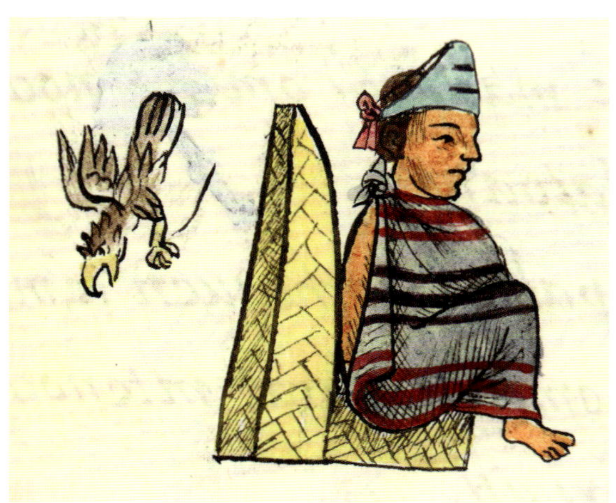

FIGURE 10 | **Master of Complex Skin Coloring.** First creator couple, who made the calendar. From Bernardino de Sahagún, *Florentine Codex* (ca. 1575–77), bk. 4, fol. 246v (detail). Florence, Biblioteca Medicea Laurenziana.

FIGURE 11 | **Master of Both Traditions.** Cuauhtemoc. From Bernardino de Sahagún, *Florentine Codex* (ca. 1575–77), bk. 8, fol. 254r (detail). Florence, Biblioteca Medicea Laurenziana.

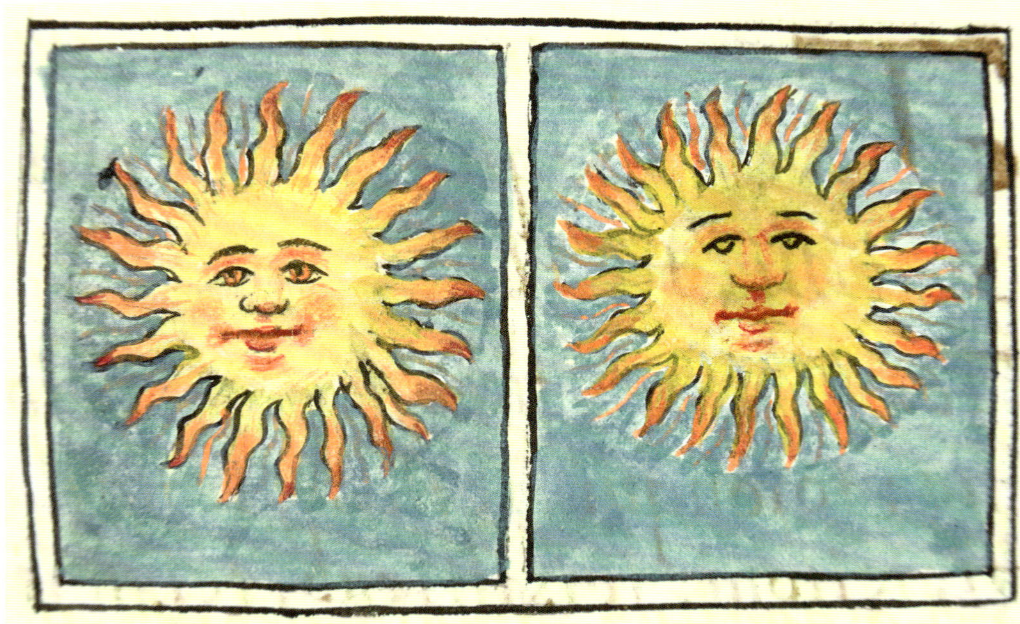

eclipse (fig. 12). The eclipse is personified by means of a graphic resource that divides the representation into two parallel pictures in which two highly similar suns are painted. Each sun is yellow, with a round, benign human face; each emits numerous rays bearing wavy contours with orange tips on the perimeter; and each has full red lips and flesh-colored cheeks. The only differences are that the sun on the left has vibrant, open eyes and seems to be smiling, while the one on the right has closed eyelids and a neutral expression. In this way, the painter represents the eclipse—the passing absence of the sun's presence—by closing the right sun's eyes. In its apparent simplicity, the representation of the eclipse implies a complex intellectual operation that revisits the fundamental concept discussed earlier concerning paintings as *ixiptlah*—in other words, following Viveiros de Castro, paintings as activated subjects who possess their own point of view.[64]

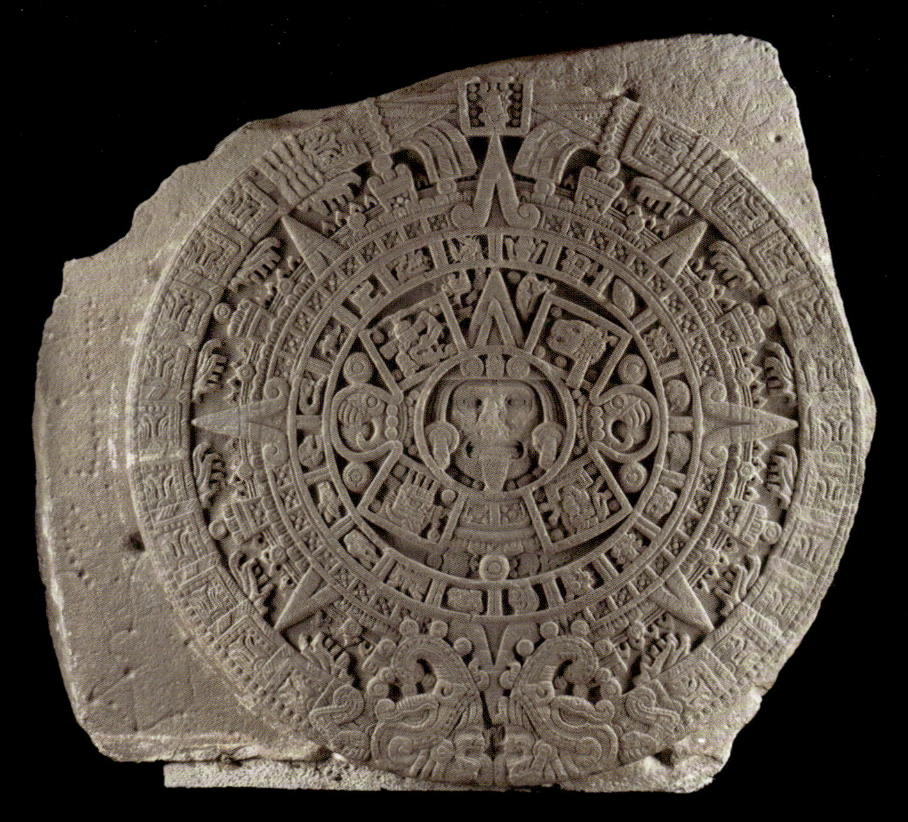

The stylistic transformation that this image represents is significant. In the Mesoamerican past, the sun was depicted in a completely different way. For example, the renowned Sun Stone shows the face of the sun as an indomitable warrior, with lips parted to reveal his teeth and a sacrificial flint knife instead of a tongue; the fierceness of his fixed gaze is reinforced by parallel lines that echo the contour of his eyes (fig. 13). Two concentric circles frame his face with day signs and a series of groups of five dots, representing precious *chalchihuites,* or greenstones. There are exactly eight solar rays, each of which is rendered as an inverted *V* shape.

By transforming the ancient face of the sun and the shape of his rays, the Master of Both Traditions literally created a new subject: the planet-king of the new Christian age in Mesoamerica.[65] The master who invented this iconic figure had no way of anticipating that his sun, with its benign face and curved rays, would continue through history to the remote future of the twenty-first century as an unequivocal symbol of indigenous presence in Mexico. The same figure remains alive in the paintings on *amate* (bark) paper of the Nahuas of Puebla, Guerrero, and Central Mexico and has been copied and reused by artisans throughout Mexico who are likely unaware that it comes from book 7 of the *Florentine Codex* and that it was created by a great artist in the sixteenth century.

Figure 14 presents a very interesting example in which the Master of Both Traditions juxtaposes these two pictorial styles in a single image. This painting, from book 3, illustrates a mythical passage from the life of Quetzalcoatl, the ancient ruler of Tollan, the great city that served as a model of civilization for the Aztecs. In fact, in Mexica historiography, Tollan is both a royal city and a mythical prototype whose foundational history and decadence served as an exegetic resource to prefigure the fall of Mexico-Tenochtitlan at the hands of the Spaniards. In figure 14 we witness an important moment in this history of the fall of Tollan and end of Quetzalcoatl's reign. An old man (who is the fearful god Tezcatlipoca in disguise) offers the ruler Quetzalcoatl the intoxicating brew known as pulque, which, according to custom, Quetzalcoatl is prohibited from ingesting. Despite the fact that the outcome of this saga is not represented in the painting, we know that Quetzalcoatl drinks the pulque and in a drunken state commits a series of transgressions; these culminate in his abdication and exile from the kingdom in the direction of the mythical place of writing, known as *tlillan tlapallan,* where he immolates himself and from where it is believed he will return someday in the future.[66] In the representation of this passage, the Master of Both Traditions decided to paint the disguised Tezcatlipoca in a Renaissance style: the concern with the body and its *contrapposto* stance, the movement and volume of the drapery, and the old man's wavy hair were all prevalent in European painting of the period. In contrast, Quetzalcoatl has different bodily proportions and

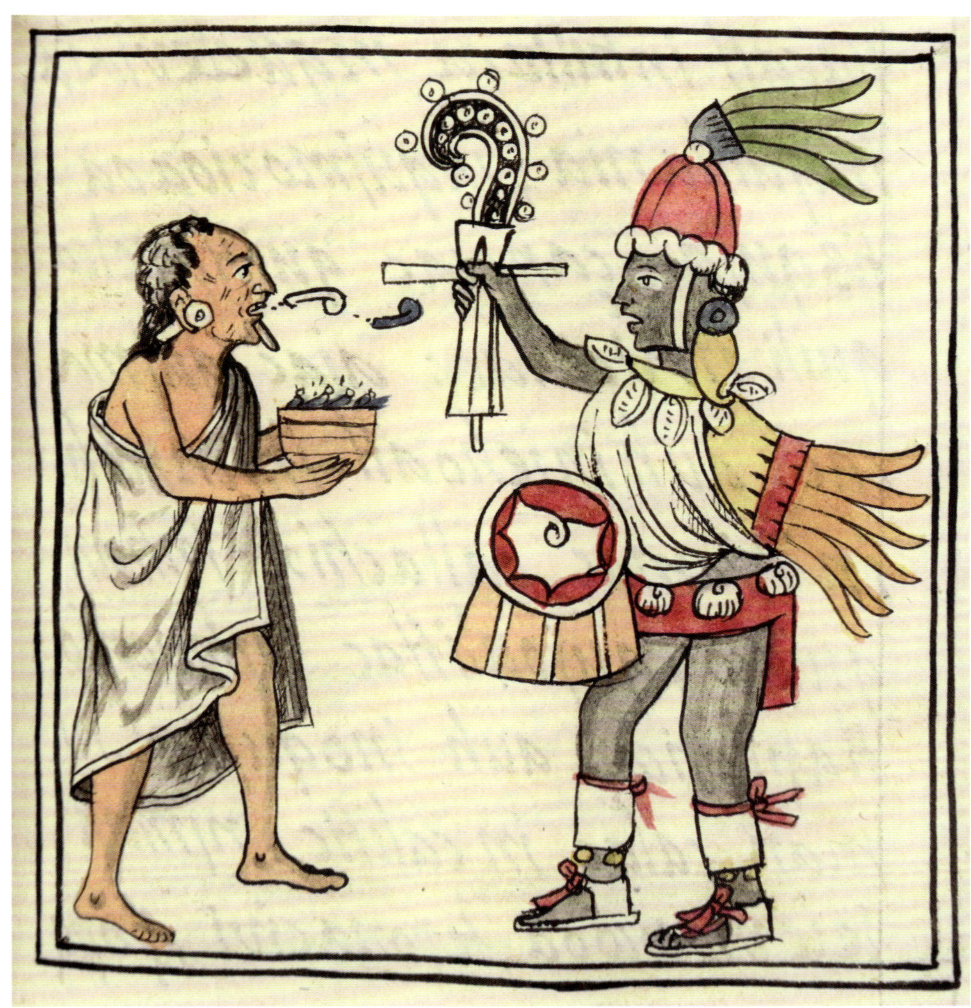

FIGURE 14 | **Master of Both Traditions.** Quetzalcoatl and Tezcatlipoca. From Bernardino de Sahagún, *Florentine Codex* (ca. 1575–77), bk. 3, fol. 213r (detail). Florence, Biblioteca Medicea Laurenziana.

treatment: he is quite tall and much more rigid, with broad limbs, and is painted with flat colors, evoking the conventions and forms from the indigenous tradition of the past. Through the contrast in styles, the Master of Both Traditions denotes two different times: the Mexica past that assimilated ancient Tollan (represented by Quetzalcoatl) and the present in New Spain (represented by Tezcatlipoca as an old man). The painter transforms this image into a window on mythical time; the events of the past that brought about the fall of Tollan prefigure the present in New Spain with the fall of Mexico-Tenochtitlan at the hands of the Europeans.

Who is this painting intended to address? What are the series of social relations implicit in it? Who would have been able to understand the nuances of this image as a representation of contrasting times and the presence of prefigured histories? The complexity and depth of the *in tlilli in tlapalli* tradition as a method of recording history with images is just beginning to be revealed. The following discussion delves into the extraordinary concept and technique of color literally being endowed with the luminous energy of the paintings.

ANALYSES IDENTIFYING COLORS

On the basis of the chemical/analytical study I conducted with the chemists at the Università di Firenze, the original colors in the *Florentine Codex* can be divided into two opposing groups. Transparent tones are of an organic nature and were obtained from plants, flowers, and insects; I will refer to these as colorants or dyes. Colors on saturated surfaces were identified as minerals; I will refer to these as pigments. The colorants and most of the pigments were of Mesoamerican origin. We found only one European pigment, minium (red lead), applied to the paintings in the *Florentine Codex*.[67]

A key finding of the research on color in the paintings is that the artists used colorants made from plants and mineral pigments to produce the same color. In other words, the purpose of the organic colorants was not to obtain colors different from what could be obtained from minerals. Thus it is apparent that their use in images was related not directly to their tone but rather to their materiality and provenance, implying that colors had a specific significance based on their raw material and their natural state.

REDS

We identified the use of two organic colorants (*nocheztli* [cochineal] and *achiotl* [annatto]) and two red mineral pigments (*tlahuitl* [hematite] and cinnabar). Artists employed the red colorant *nocheztli* most frequently (see fig. 5). *Nocheztli*'s natural color, similar to that of blood, changes to orange with the addition of an acidic substance and to purple or brown with the addition of an alkali such as lime water.[68] As can be seen in figure 14, the cap, sash, and inner part of Quetzalcoatl's shield are painted using *nocheztli* in its red tonality, while the feathers decorating the side of his arm and the strips hanging from his shield are painted with the colorant in its orange tone. The white cape of the old man is shaded with alkaline *nocheztli* that produced a brown hue. *Nocheztli* was identified through FT-IR (Fourier Transform Infrared Spectroscopy) based on its characteristic carminic acid compound; this compound appears in all three cases.

In the *Florentine Codex,* specific paintings contain a mixture of an unidentified red colorant and a mineral red pigment. In figure 15, for example, the goddess Coatlicue, mother of the gods at the beginning of time and symbol of the earth itself, is painted brick red, which in the analyses was determined not to be *nocheztli* and is probably *achiotl.*[69] The Nahua treatise does mention two more colorants, one of which is *achiotl* (Lat. *Bixa orellana*), described as "light red"; and another produced with bark from the *uitzquauitl,* known as *palo de brasil* or Mexican logwood (Lat. *Haematoxylum brasiletto*) and used primarily to dye cloth.[70] Scientific

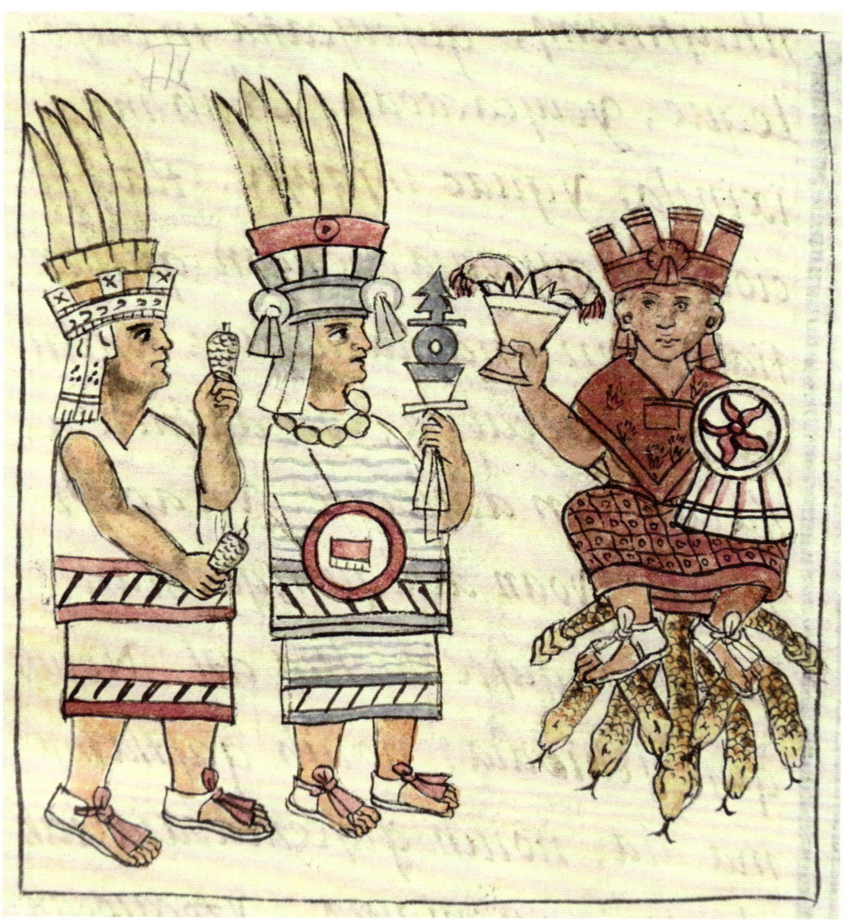

FIGURE 15 | **Coatlicue**. From Bernardino de Sahagún, *Florentine Codex* (ca. 1575–77), bk. 1, fol. 18v (detail). Florence, Biblioteca Medicea Laurenziana.

studies also indicate that the color used to paint Coatlicue contains a high percentage of iron, suggesting that the organic colorant had been mixed with a mineral based on iron oxide (possibly hematite). Figure 16 is the day sign *xochitl* (flower), on the page from the *tonalpohualli,* the ritual calendar, in book 4. The calendar is composed of twenty day signs and thirteen numerals combined to result in a total of 260 days. As seen in the detail of the image, a brighter red layer identified as the mineral cinnabar (mercury sulfide), also known as vermilion, was applied on top of

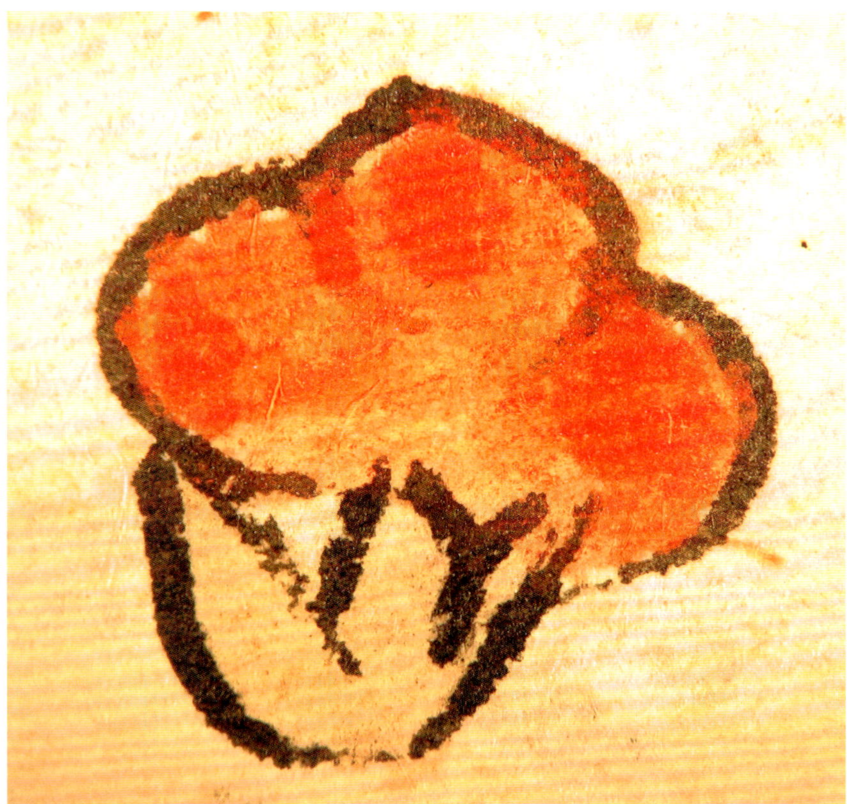

the colorant, which is *nocheztli*. The addition of cinnabar is also found on the red maws of the day sign *cipactli* (crocodile). It is interesting that these two day signs are repainted with cinnabar, because they are the alpha and omega of the ritual calendar: *cipactli* is the first day and *xochitl* the last. In all of the above-mentioned examples, the addition of a mineral pigment to the colorant did not modify the red chromatic value, so its presence could only be ascertained via chemical analysis.

The Nahua treatise records only one red mineral pigment, *tlahuitl*.[71] The painting that illustrates it shows in two parallel images the *tlahuitl* next to a white mineral called *tizatl* (calcium sulfate), both in their natural state (fig. 17). The *tlahuitl* is represented as compact cylindrical pieces that have been extracted from a cave interior; the *tizatl* is a mudlike clay found in lake bottoms and then heated to produce the pigment. According to the indigenous worldview, both extraction spots (the cave and the lake bottom) are places of access to the underworld, an alternate space governed by another sort of time, the dwelling place of the ancestors that connects to the wet, heavy, feminine, dark matter from the time of creation.[72] The *tlahuitl* is thus a red mineral codified as a heavy, telluric material from the underworld. It is likely that *tlahuitl* is hematite. However, cinnabar is also a mineral obtained from mines; in this way, both share the same telluric associations.[73] In opposition to the mineral *tlahuitl,* the two red colorants (*nocheztli* and *achiotl*) are manufactured from an insect that lives on prickly pear pads and from the seeds of a fruit, respectively. Both colorants grow on the earth's surface thanks to sunlight, and in the Nahua vision of the world they pertain to another cosmic sphere: the hot, luminous, lightweight, and masculine solar world of above. Alfredo López Austin comments that the division into two types of material—mineral and organic—was present at the origin of the world, when the gods made land emerge as a huge cosmic crocodile, called Cipactli, from the dark bottom of the primordial waters and split it into two: "The gods emerging from the upper half of her body were hot, dry, and luminous; those emerging from the lower half were cold, humid, and dark."[74]

Creation was a process in which the different forces from the two halves of Cipactli were combined in different proportions. In the same way, the painters blended mineral pigments and organic colorants in a ritual action similar to what was carried out by the gods at the origin of time. The goddess Coatlicue, as the earth itself, is painted with both substances: the mineral from the moist, dark, creative earth and the organic material from the sunlight that makes plants grow. Together, the substances form a complete, powerful being. The day signs *cipactli* and *xochitl,* as signs of time and the beginning and end of the Nahua day count, also contain both

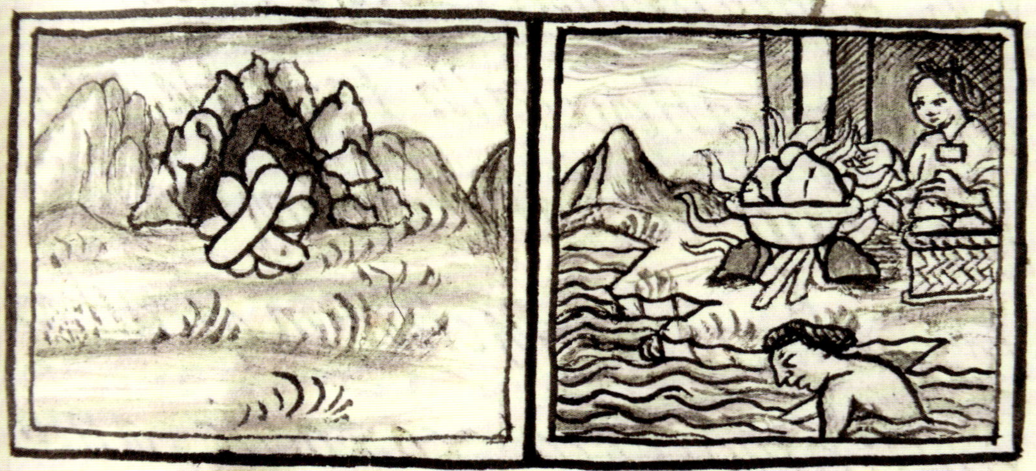

materials, because time is defined as the result of the alternation of these dark and luminous forces, whose proportions shift according to the time of day and the season of the year.[75]

Artists employed the same combination of red colorants and pigments to paint the background of the murals that decorate the royal tombs in the Zapotec cities of Monte Albán (ca. AD 550–650) and Suchilquitongo (ca. AD 800–900). It has been proposed that this mixture symbolically marks the tombs as caves of origin and that cinnabar was used to indicate "another time," that of the ancestors.[76] As a result, the red gives the eternal time of the gods a color and with it a special luminous force; in addition, either colorants or minerals could be used, depending on the proportions of lightweight and solar or moist, heavy, and telluric matter that each possessed.[77]

The other red pigment that we identified is minium, red lead or lead oxide from Europe. It was so commonly used in medieval illuminated manuscripts that those paintings were called *miniatures* from *miniare* in

Latin, which means "to color with red."[78] Minium's use in the *Florentine Codex* is specific: it appears on images that describe or represent the colonial present as a new era. For example, in figure 12, the two suns of the eclipse are colored with a yellow dye that could be either of the two colorants mentioned in the Nahua treatise: *zacatlaxcalli* (Lat. *Cuscuta tinctoria*) or *xochipalli* (yellow cosmos; Lat. *Cosmos sulphureus*),[79] but we determined that the orange color on the tips of the rays is the mineral minium. Other representations of the new sun exist in book 7 and, significantly, all of them have minium. The European red mineral on the sun's rays served the painters in rendering the sun of the new era, that of Christian Mesoamerica. In fact, for the Nahuas the sun not only was the planet that emitted light but also represented the lord that determined and controlled time. Thus, the sun was equated with Xiuhtecuhtli, "Lord Turquoise," the God of Time, and the *tlatoani* (rulers) were the *ixiptlah*, or incarnations, of Xiuhtecuhtli.[80] With the arrival of the Spaniards and the advent of the Christian faith, Christ came to occupy this central position.[81]

THE DEATH OF MOCTEZUMA IN FULL COLOR

A painting from book 12 offers another powerful example of how color is used to mark different times and spaces (fig. 18). The painting shows the most significant event in the war that marked the end of the Mexica era: the deaths of the ruler of Mexico-Tenochtitlan, Moctezuma, and the ruler of its sister city Tlatelolco, Itzcuauhtzin, at the hands of the Spaniards. The indigenous history of book 12 tells how after the battle of Toxcatl, in which the Mexicas and the Tlatelolcas managed to expel the foreign contingent, the Spaniards, who had taken Moctezuma and Itzcuauhtzin prisoner, killed them and then discarded their bodies by tossing them into the Grand Canal.[82]

The image corresponding to this passage stands out in particular; to fully understand it, one must observe the painters' symbolic codification deployed through the luminosity and the raw materials used to make the colors. Two Spaniards hold Itzcuauhtzin by his hands and feet to throw him into the Grand Canal; Moctezuma has already been cast in and he floats in the dark, agitated waters. It is noteworthy that the upper half of

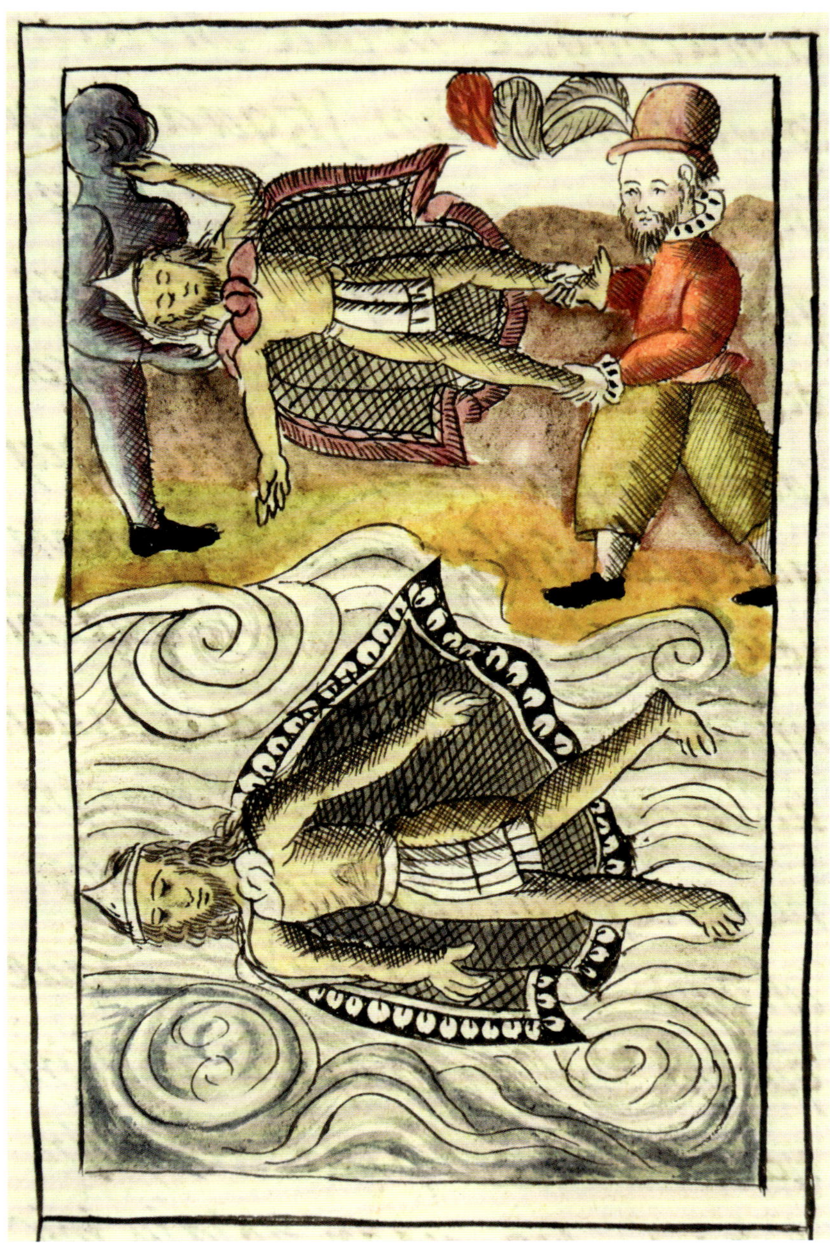

FIGURE 18 | **Moctezuma dead in the waters of the Grand Canal.** From Bernardino de Sahagún, *Florentine Codex* (ca. 1575–77), bk. 12, fol. 447v (detail). Florence, Biblioteca Medicea Laurenziana.

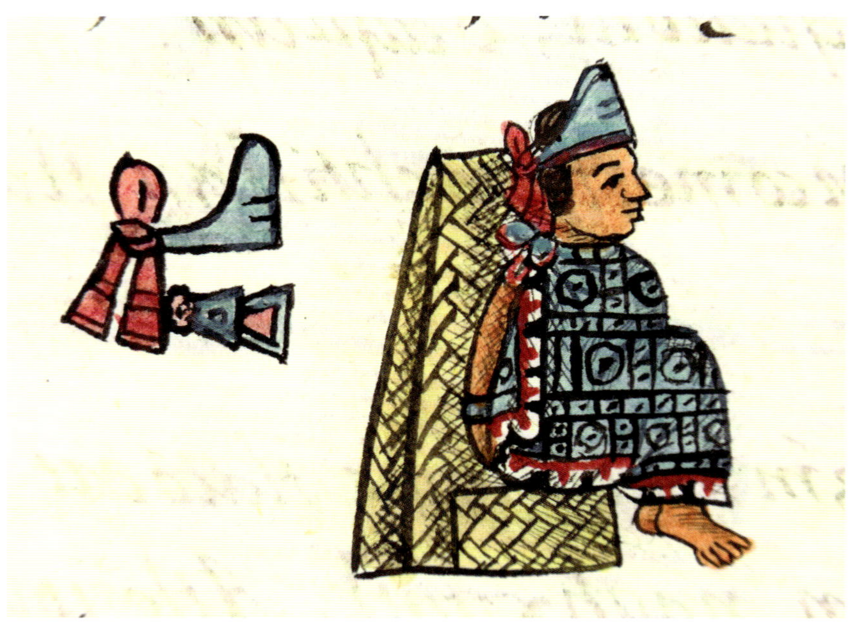

FIGURE 19 | Moctezuma with his *xiuhtlapalli tilmahtli* (blue royal cape). From Bernardino de Sahagún, *Florentine Codex* (ca. 1575–77), bk. 8, fol. 252v (detail). Florence, Biblioteca Medicea Laurenziana.

the painting is colored with bright, saturated tones, while the lower part is rendered with more diluted colors. The contrast relates to two historical facts. Above are the victors and therefore their "color covering" is vibrant and strong. Below them lies the Mexica ruler, already dead, beginning his journey to the underworld submerged in water. Like a sun without strength, his colors are dark and weak. The solar world is now occupied by the victors in war, the Spaniards, and the aquatic underworld is inhabited by the vanquished, represented here by Moctezuma.[83]

The use of blue in this image clearly demonstrates how the Nahua created meaning through the contrast in color. In the Nahua worldview, blue is associated with the center of fire (which has an intense blue color) as a mover of time, and it denotes something precious. The armor-clad soldier in figure 18 is painted blue; this tone, identified with the colorant indigo and referred to in the Nahua treatise as *tlaceuilli* (Lat. *Indigofera suffruticosa*), has a brilliant appearance, which possibly imitated a metallic reflection.[84] The blue of the armor contrasts with the grayish tone of the water, also identified as indigo but applied in diluted form and mixed with another colorant to make the tone more opaque. Similarly, the royal symbols worn by the Aztec rulers are given special treatment. Equivalent to crowns worn by European kings, the sovereigns' *xiuhuitzolli* (diadems), normally characterized by their turquoise-blue color, are here deprived of color. The *xiuhtlapalli tilmahtli* (blue royal capes), which were made of fine cotton dyed with indigo in a net design and embellished with turquoise appliqué, are likewise painted with indigo, but in a dull, flat tone lacking any sheen.[85] Comparing the color of Moctezuma's royal cape—rendered, as just noted, with an indigo colorant in a dull tone—to that in his portrait as the Lord of Mexico in book 8 confirms the purposeful manipulation of color in the painting of his death (fig. 19; cf. fig. 18).

Scientific analyses enable us to identify the presence of palygorskite clay in the turquoise-blue colors (fig. 20; see figs. 12, 19) and in the very brilliant light green, probably *quiltic* (Maya green), used in book 9 to paint the quetzal feathers (see figs. 2, 6, 7). The color *texotli* (Maya blue) has been made from this white clay since at least the Classic period in the Maya area (AD 400–500).[86] The technique to make it requires fixing the blue colorant of indigo in the crystalline structure of the clay by heating it in water. Palygorskite clay can be found only on the Yucatán Peninsula; therefore, the raw material to make the *texotli* and *quiltic,* as well as the ready-made colors, had to be imported to Mexico City.

Based on its origin (the rich lands of southern Mesoamerica) and its mixed composition (made from a mineral and an organic colorant), *texotli* is a special pigment that possesses both types of cosmic matter: solar and telluric. It is employed in the *Florentine Codex* extensively to symbolize everything that is precious. The backgrounds representing the sky in all of the images of the sun, moon, and stars in book 7 are painted with *texotli* (see figs. 12, 20).[87] It was used to paint royal capes, diadems, and jewelry worn by the *tlatoani* (rulers) of Mexico-Tenochtitlan, Tlatelolco, Texcoco, and Huxutla. The fine quetzal feathers in book 9 are colored with

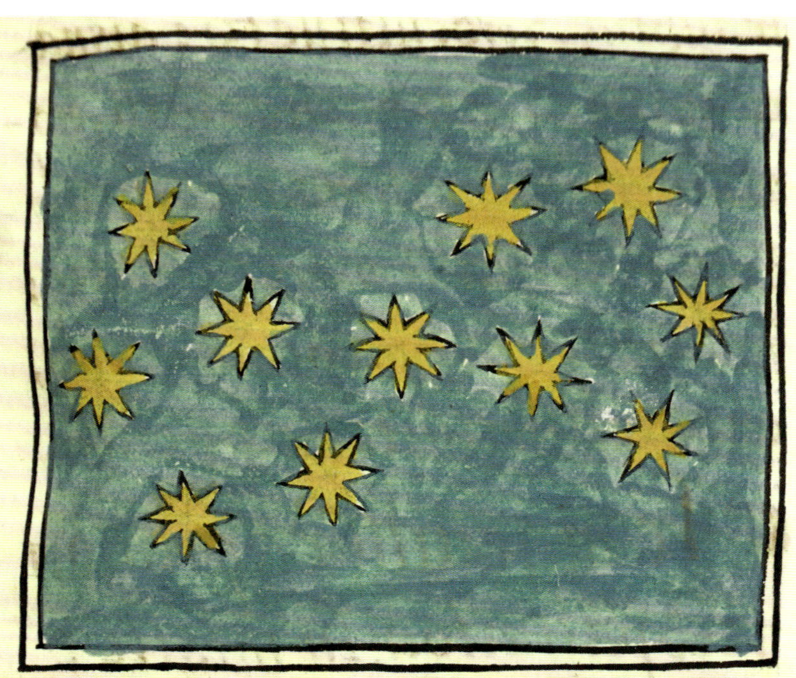

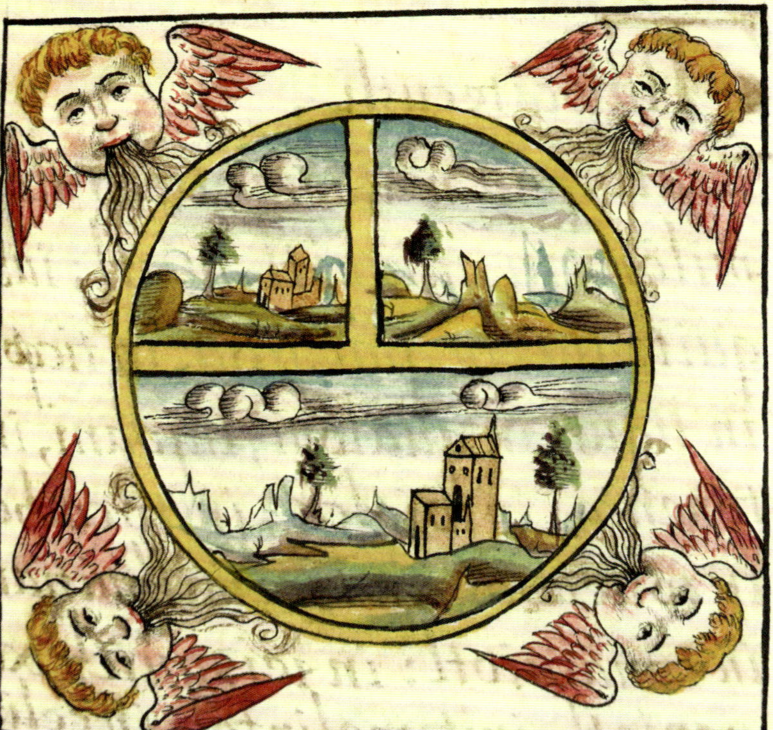

a mixture of *texotli* and a yellow colorant to make *quiltic* (see figs. 2, 7); the distant mountains in the landscapes of the rich lands in the south of New Spain are painted with *texotli* to explore aerial perspective (see fig. 4); and the crystalline waters of creation are painted with this precious color.

Yet, as discussed above, the brilliance of blue is muted in the image of Moctezuma and Itzcuauhtzin (see fig. 18). Painters transformed the turquoise of the capes into a dull gray and covered the rulers' bodies in dark, swirling waters lacking any sheen. In this way, the painters not only portrayed the historical event—the death of Moctezuma at the hands of the enemy—but also interpreted it: the representative of the Mexica sun had been defeated and lost his solar luminosity and heat. The Mexica *tlatoani* did not consummate his destiny as a triumphant warrior who at death went to the House of the Sun, where the multicolored birds, the avatars of defeated warriors, dwelled. Instead, once defeated, Moctezuma and Itzcuauhtzin were beings in the dark, aquatic, telluric, and lunar underworld.

Earlier I remarked upon the use of red to denote two times and two places, and such usage also applies to the image of Moctezuma's death. The border and knot of Itzcuauhtzin's cape are painted in *nocheztli*. This red contrasts with the orange color of the shirt and the feathers in the hat of the other figure, a Spaniard, identified as minium. The two reds signify different places and times: minium, which came from Europe, represents the present dominated by the Spaniards who won the war, while *nocheztli*, from Mesoamerica, represents the indigenous past.

Thus, by manipulating the contrasts between saturated and diluted colors and by using *nocheztli* and minium reds, the painting displays two temporalities: the indigenous era that was coming to an end and the Spanish age that was beginning its control by killing the representative of the Mexica sun, the emperor Moctezuma.

The use of contrasts based on luminosity and strength of colors to produce figures possessing distinct symbolic status is key to Nahua painting. For example, the representation of Paynal (as well as other gods from the Mexica pantheon in the same book) is painted with diluted colors (see fig. 3). The elements of the attire most altered in terms of color are those of greatest importance, and based on what is known of his insignia they should have been tinted with *texotli* (Maya blue) and *quiltic* (Maya green). However, Paynal's royal cape is painted light gray and his turquoise mosaic shield is devoid of color. Perhaps in other times and under other circumstances both insignia would have been painted with *texotli*—which as we know from the description in book 1 is essential to the identity of the god—and would have had all of that color's strength. The quetzal feathers he wears in his headdress are painted with a dry green that in no way resembles the *quiltic* of the quetzal feathers crafted by the *amanteca* (feather artists) in book 9 (see fig. 7). Why was it necessary to proceed in this way, leaving Paynal stripped of *texotli* and *quiltic,* the two colors symbolic of preciousness, both made with Maya blue? Why are the gods on the six folios depicting the Aztec pantheon painted with colors lacking brilliance and vibrancy?

To analyze this representation of Paynal, we must return to the concept of *ixiptlah* discussed earlier. We should bear in mind, as López Austin observed, that the *ixiptlah* received the luminous force of the numen and took on form through the "covering."[88] These *ixiptlah* figures *in tlilli in tlapalli*—the Nahua notion of wisdom defined as what is inscribed in books with black ink and colors—possess a luminous force given by their "covering" as well as a shape that identifies them. I have demonstrated that the covering refers to both shape and colors and that these are composed of two raw materials from the creation: lightweight solar matter from colorants made from plants; and dark, wet, lunar matter from mineral pigments. Furthermore, in accord with these ideas, *ixiptlah* paintings have been activated as subjects and possess their own point of view. Conceived in these terms, the very act of creating these images cannot be separated from the ritual action that gave them a sense of reality.[89] Johannes Neurath, in his study of the production of Huichol yarn paintings in Mexico today, comments that the famed artist Juan Ríos Martínez "suffered from the anger of the gods represented in his pictures" because "the figures that, according to the logic of Western art, would simply be represented in the yarn paintings did not cease to 'be' deities." Images in Huichol art, according to Neurath, "are powerful people and they must be venerated." Curiously, this is always true when it comes to exceptional paintings, in other words, "inspired works." In fact, Ríos Martínez decided to stop making what he regarded as "great art" and instead concentrated on works using simple techniques. Those works could be sold as folk art to tourists because they did not possess the power of the vision that his earlier images had.[90]

The phenomenon experienced by Ríos Martínez can explain the absence of power in the colors of the paintings of the gods from the Mexica pantheon in book 1 of the *Florentine Codex*. The *toltecaye* did not wish to make powerful images. In the sixteenth century they could no longer continue venerating them as they had done in the past, so they did not paint them with their original colors, particularly the *texotli* and the *quiltic,* and in this way, they painted inoffensive beings.[91]

However, other paintings exist that contain the complete potency of color representing the indigenous world in New Spain. It is important to show them here to fully understand the notion of *in tlilli in tlapalli* in the *Florentine Codex.*

THE RESTORATION OF THE EARTH AND SUN

Figure 20 shows two paintings from book 7 that are intimately linked symbolically and visually. According to the texts in Nahuatl and Spanish, the lower image illustrates the four winds produced by the god Quetzalcoatl from the four corners of the world. The east wind, Ehecatl Tlalocan, was benevolent; the wind that blew from Mictlampa in the north was fierce; the one from Ciuatlampa in the west was relatively inoffensive; and the wind Uiztlampa Ehecatl, which blew from the south, was destructive. The winds are represented here as four angelic cherubs who blow with force. In the center of the painting—and much more prominent—is the representation of Earth. The painter, the Master of Both Traditions, used as a model a medieval image of the *imago mundi* created for the encyclopedic compendium *Etymologiae* by Isidore of Seville in the seventh century. Isidore's *imago mundi* represented scientific and cosmographic advances, incorporating material from the Bible: Earth is shown as a sphere, surrounded by the ocean and divided into the three regions of the world that were known at that time: Asia, Europe, and Africa. This image of the *imago mundi* was widely known across the world including, by this time, in New Spain.[92]

The painting in the *Florentine Codex* provides an interesting transmutation of the indigenous conception. For the Nahuas, the myth of the creation and the re-creation of the earth in each cosmic era was fundamental. In the indigenous vision of the past, history was cyclic, and there had been five cosmic eras, called "suns," until the Mexica era prior to the conquest. That latter era was known as the Fifth Sun.

The basic precepts of this history are as follows: the gods made land rise from the deep waters of the primordial sea. The land was envisaged as a huge cosmic crocodile known as Cipactli-Tlaltecuhtli, "Cayman Lord of the Earth."[93] Later, the creator gods, Quetzalcoatl and Tezcatlipoca, penetrated the four corners of this earth monster and met in the middle,[94] where they were transformed into two enormous serpents that intertwined and rose up to elevate the sky.[95] Then the gods were transformed again into the great dual cosmic tree in the center of the earth, whose branches are the sky, whose trunk is the earth's surface, and whose roots are the underworld. This tree is also known as Tamoanchan.[96] Because the earth was penetrated from the four corners, it was built as a space with four regions: east, north, west, and south. The cosmic tree in the center supporting the vault of the sky ensures that the sun can travel all the regions of the earth and thus give rise to time and begin the days and years of the east, north, west, and south (the calendar). The cosmic tree can also be represented as the four pillars or trees at the corners of the world.[97]

In the image by the Master of Both Traditions, Cipactli-Tlaltecuhtli is transformed into the sphere of the *imago mundo,* to which, ingeniously, the four cosmic regions have been incorporated via the four Ehecatl [wind god]-angels that blow from the corners. These angels have taken the structural and symbolic place of the four cosmic pillars that uphold the skies.[98]

It is important that the angels be avatars of Quetzalcoatl, one of the creator gods who forms the tree of Tamoanchan with his energy. The wings of the Ehecatl-angels are painted with *nocheztli* and not with minium red, reinforcing the idea that they are part of the Nahua world. The landscapes on the interior of the sphere recall other views in the *Florentine Codex* that show the countryside and the new construction of religious and civil establishments in New Spain. This painting, therefore, illustrates the restoration of Cipactli-Tlaltecuhtli in the new Christian period: the union of a circle, which represents the sky, and a square, which represents the earth, to form the number eight.[99] In the center, the mystical figure of Christ or the cross stands as the Mesoamerican cosmic tree. In this sense, this composition merges both visual and symbolic traditions.[100]

The upper image depicts special stars that, grouped together, make an *S* shape. These are described in the Nahuatl text as "apart" from the other constellations: "[These] were apart; they appeared by themselves, shining and shimmering. And for this reason were they called *S*-shaped stars—that they were similar to and very much like a [kind of maize] tortilla which was made, or an amaranth seed tortilla. [These] were, at both ends, twisted and rounded over. They were eaten on the day Xochitl, everywhere, in each house."[101]

From the preceding it is important to highlight that this group of stars appeared on *xochitl* days. Also key is the emphasis on the stars' *S* shape in the sky. The painting, in fact, attempts to show this phenomenon (see fig. 20). To better understand the stars' significance one must take into account that the day *ce xochitl* (one flower) was celebrated with a great fiesta of song and dance, which at times lasted up to forty days and in which all the nobles, as well as Moctezuma, participated. During the celebration, the gods were favorable and granted boons, people feasted, and "all the people rejoiced completely."[102] It was precisely on this day that everyone danced and sang—and, it seems, also when the *S*-shaped stars appeared on their own.[103]

The text accompanying the image refers to the last day of the divinatory calendar, *xochitl,* when a cycle of time was completed. Apparently, this completion is also signaled by the appearance of the *S*-shaped constellation on *xochitl* days. Thus, the Master of Both Traditions has established an intimate relationship between image and text; the New Earth (the *imago mundi*) emerged at the end of a cycle of time (the past era, depicted by the stars). By placing the starry vault of the sky above the figure of the earth, he manages to portray the two halves of the New Earth, as the gods had done to Cipactli at the moment of creation, and in this way he has made the new cosmos appear.[104] To this end, the master also used the Nahua codes governing color. He painted the sky with blue identified as the precious *texotli* (Maya blue). In addition, he colored the stars in a special way; when they are seen in the original document, they possess a brilliance and color so vibrant that they seem to be made of gold leaf. We analyzed this color, hoping to find traces of a metal; however, identification analyses showed that they are painted with a yellow colorant. According to information on yellows in the Nahua treatise, it must be *xochipalli* (flower which dyes), known as "fine yellow" and described as a substance "for giving luster" and "for making things radiant."[105]

The stars that twinkle in the original manuscript as if they were rendered in gold reinforce the idea I suggested earlier: that the *toltecaye* participated from their own tradition in the debate on pictorial materials undertaken by Pliny the Elder and then revisited by contemporary artists during the Renaissance. In his book 35, on colors, Pliny dedicates a section to gold and silver, which are also discussed in moral terms. While sculptures in true gold are regarded as "curiosities," the skill of imitating gold and above all its luminosity is considered a creative value.[106] What's more, as in all of the paintings in the *Florentine Codex*, the very materiality of the colorant with which they were made possesses an ulterior significance. As mentioned above, the *xochipalli* is translated as "flower which dyes" and the *S*-shaped stars are associated with the fiesta of *ce xochitl* (one flower), when the people danced, sang, and ate folded corn tortillas. As Berenice Alcántara Rojas has pointed out, the power of flowers in indigenous pre-Hispanic and colonial fiestas was that of manifesting the luminous, hot power of the creator gods. This world, called "flower world," was one form of Tamoanchan, "the place of the tree in blossom at the center of space and time."[107]

Tamoanchan, according to López Austin, is one of the most important locations in creation myths. It is "the place where the most important functions of the cosmic mechanism took place." It is at the origin of the world and also in the present because it is the "sacred union of two times, the today of this world and the forever present of the divine realm."[108] The Master of Both Traditions represents Tamoanchan in book 7 by means of twinkling stars, made with flower-based paint and twisted into an *S* like the braided, twisted energy that made possible the transfer of essences through the trunk of Tamoanchan. This vision of the *texotli* blue sky and *xochipalli* yellow stars arranged in an *S* recalls an outstanding moment in the history of the foundation of Mexico-Tenochtitlan. In fact, López Austin refers to the intertwining of the opposite forces of creation represented by water (blue) and fire (yellow) as "the miraculous appearances of the *malinalli*," which marks the union of the time of the gods and the time of humankind.[109] In this sense, the emphasis in texts on the stars forming an *S* like tortillas folded back on themselves becomes understandable: it is the image of the place where the blue and the yellow waters of the Mexica myths of creation cross, and the opposing forces that generate creation are clearly indicated in this way. The Master of Both Traditions produces in his painting a play of mirrors replicating and multiplying the primordial creation to shape the present of New Spain. From the present, the painting evokes the foundation of Mexico-Tenochtitlan in the past era, when the "aquatic bonfire" appeared at the intersection of the blue and yellow waters, which made it possible for the Mexicas to know they had found the place predestined by the gods for their city.[110] In this way, the master, paraphrasing words used by the Nahua painters of the *Anales de Juan Bautista*, has "made appear" and "has shown" us the *ixiptlah* of the very creation of the New Earth, called New Spain, from a Tamoanchan that managed with its power to merge the history and geography of Europe and Mesoamerica.

Despite the fact that death pulled down its dark, heavy veil over the Nahuas by means of the epidemic that brought an end to nearly two-thirds of the indigenous population in Central Mexico in 1576, the artists of the *Florentine Codex* held on to the ancient tradition of the *toltecaye*. With their art they repainted the world and made the new land and new era appear with all the power that their artistry permitted. The *toltecaye* of both traditions created a new pictorial style, which from their own indigenous tradition deployed the skills and visual habits of their contemporaries, the artists of the Renaissance, and with this the *toltecaye* established a place for their artistic tradition in their own time. Thanks to their profound knowledge of pictorial materials, they were dedicated to conjuring the devastation and "making the world appear" for future generations through their age-old practice of painting the subjects of history—not its objects—with the colors of the earth and the sun. Their images, like everything created by the gods, possess the same formula as the cosmos: a combination of graded intensities of light, heat, and weightlessness, blended with a range of darkness, moisture, and heaviness. In New Spain, the *toltecaye* explained this practice to themselves and their contemporaries using the same terms Pliny the Elder used to defend the creativity of the great Greek artist Apelles; thus, the intermediary state between "ritual" and "art" still observed in indigenous production today was sheltered by a humanist idea. Using colors empowered by their raw materials, the *toltecaye* of the *Florentine Codex* imitated the gods in Tamoanchan by making their world appear for us.

Notes

1.　[A three-volume facsimile was published as Fray Bernardino de Sahagún, *Historia general de las cosas de Nueva España* (Mexico City: Secretaría de Gobernación, 1979), and a twelve-volume English translation of the Nahuatl is available: Fray Bernardino de Sahagún, *Florentine Codex: General History of the Things of New Spain,* trans. Arthur J. O. Anderson and Charles E. Dibble (Santa Fe, N.Mex.: School of American Research, 1950–69; reprint, Salt Lake City: University of Utah, 1970–82). *–Trans.*]

2.　Alfredo López Austin, "Estudio introductorio a Bernardino de Sahagún," in Fray Bernardino de Sahagún, *Historia general de las cosas de Nueva España,* edited and with an introduction, glossary, and notes by Alfredo López Austin and Josefina García Quintana (Mexico City: Conaculta, 2002), 1:37–52. José Rubén Romero Galván, "Fray Bernardino de Sahagún y la historia general de las cosas de Nueva España," in Miguel León-Portilla, ed., *Bernardino de Sahagún: Quinientos años de presencia* (Mexico City: Universidad Nacional Autónoma de México, 2002), 23.

3.　The Mexicas were the ancient inhabitants of Mexico-Tenochtitlan and were also known as the Aztecs. The Nahuatl-speaking groups in Central Mexico are called Nahuas, a term that is synonymous with the ancient Mexica and Aztec people. It can also refer to modern-day Nahuatl speakers.

4.　Fray Bernardino de Sahagún, *Historia general de las cosas de Nueva España,* edited and with an introduction, glossary, and notes by Alfredo López Austin and Josefina García Quintana (Mexico City: Conaculta, 2002), 1:130. Marina Garone Gravier identifies seven scribes in her study of the hands of the writers. See Marina

Garone Gravier, "Sahagún's Codex and Book Design in the Indigenous Context," in Gerhard Wolf and Joseph Connors, eds., *Colors between Two Worlds: The* Florentine Codex *of Bernardino de Sahagún* (Florence: Kunthistorisches Institut in Florenz, Max-Planck-Institut, 2011), 157–97.

5.	Ascensión Hernández de León-Portilla, "La historia general de Sahagún a la luz de las enciclopedias de la tradición greco-romana," in Miguel León-Portilla, ed., *Bernardino de Sahagún: Quinientos años de presencia* (Mexico City: Universidad Nacional Autónoma de México, 2002), 51.

6.	[Classical Nahuatl was primarily an oral tradition; writing was limited to pictographic-logographic signs with phonetic elements. The friars were the first to prepare Nahuatl grammars and record the language in the Latin alphabet. –*Trans.*]

7.	Sahagún, *Historia general* (2002), 1:130.

8.	The statistics are cited in José Luis Martínez Rodríguez, *El Códice Florentino y la historia general de Sahagún* (Mexico City: Archivo General de la Nación, 1982), 13.

9.	This research was possible thanks to the support of Dr. Piero Baglioni and his team of researchers from the Università di Firenze and the collaboration of the authorities from the Laurentian Library. Preliminary results were presented in Diana Magaloni Kerpel, "Painters of the New World: The Process of Making the *Florentine Codex*," in Gerhard Wolf and Joseph Connors, eds., *Colors between Two Worlds: The* Florentine Codex *of Bernardino de Sahagún* (Florence: Kunthistorisches Institut in Florenz, Max-Planck-Institut, 2011), 47–76; and in Piero Baglioni et al., "On the Nature of the Pigments of the *General History of the Things of New Spain: The* Florentine Codex," in Gerhard Wolf and Joseph Connors, eds., *Colors between Two Worlds: The* Florentine Codex *of Bernardino de Sahagún* (Florence: Kunthistorisches Institut in Florenz, Max-Planck-Institut, 2011), 79–105.

10.	Lia Markey, " 'Istoria della terra chiamata la nuova spagna': The History and Reception of Sahagún's Codex at the Medici Court," in Gerhard Wolf and Joseph Connors, eds., *Colors between Two Worlds: The* Florentine Codex *of Bernardino de Sahagún* (Florence: Kunthistorisches Institut in Florenz, Max-Planck-Institut, 2011), 210–11.

11.	For a general overview of the books, their content, and an appraisal of the texts in Spanish and Nahuatl, see López Austin, "Estudio introductorio," 1:37–55; and Arthur J. O. Anderson, "Variations on a Sahaguntine Theme" and "Sahagún's Prologues and Interpolations," in Fray Bernardino de Sahagún, *Florentine Codex: General History of the Things of New Spain,* part 1, *Introduction and Indices,* trans. Arthur J. O. Anderson and Charles E. Dibble (Santa Fe, N.Mex.: School of American Research, 1950–69; reprint, Salt Lake City: University of Utah Press, 1970–82), 3–29, 45–101.

12.	Originally, royal cosmographers were sent to record the natural history of New Spain, but it was the Nahuas who ended up producing the most complete and renowned natural history.

13.	In fact, Erasmus of Rotterdam, an author frequently read by the

Franciscans, valued the engravings of Dürer for not relying on colors in order to mimic nature perfectly. See Susan Dackerman, *Painted Prints: The Revelation of Color in Northern Renaissance and Baroque Engravings, Etchings and Woodcuts,* exh. cat. (University Park: Pennsylvania State University Press, 2002), 14.

14. Pablo Escalante, *Los códices mesoamericanos antes y después de la conquista española: Historia de un lenguaje pictográfico* (Mexico City: Fondo de Cultura Económica, 2010), 18. Escalante defines writing in images as a system of "pictograms" that are narratives and scenes, complemented by "ideograms," or sign systems, with phonetic elements. Motolinía (ca. 1543) writes of the different categories of painted books with "characters and figures" that ancient Mexicans used. Toribio de Benavente Motolinía, *Historia de los indios de la Nueva España* (Mexico City: Porrúa, 1990), 2.

15. Gisele Díaz and Alan Rodgers, *The Codex Borgia: A Full-Color Restoration of the Ancient Mexican Manuscript* (New York: Dover, 1993), 62–69.

16. Sahagún, *Historia general* (2002), 1:70.

17. Sahagún, *Florentine Codex,* book 1, p. 3. *Moteixiptlatiani* is composed of the reflexive *mo;* the indefinite *te,* which refers to persons; the verb *ixiptlatia,* which means "to substitute for someone"; and the agentive *ni.* Thus the term is translated as "he who replaces someone." Richard Andrews, Alexis Wimmer, and Michel Launay analyze this word as *ix-ip-tla-tli,* so when it becomes possessed it needs an *"b"* at the end, becoming *ixiptlab,* "his/her statue, image, representative." See entry for *ixiptlahtli* under "Repertoire," at the Nahuatl dictionary website, http://sites.estvideo.net/malinal/nahuatl .page.html. I am grateful to Karen Dakin for reviewing the translations of *ixiptlah.*

18. Sahagún, *Florentine Codex,* book 1, p. 3.

19. Alfredo López Austin, *Hombre-dios: Religión y política en el mundo náhuatl* (Mexico City: Universidad Nacional Autónoma de México, 1973), 118–20. Unless otherwise noted, translations from Spanish to English are by Debra Nagao.

20. López Austin, *Hombre-dios,* 121.

21. *Los anales de Juan Bautista,* a collective book by indigenous painters (1564–69), records the sacred images of the Virgin, Jesus, and the saints in oil painting, cornstalk paste sculpture, silver bas-relief, and mural painting as *ixiptlatzin,* in which the suffix *-tzin* is reverential. *Los anales de Juan Bautista,* trans. Luis Reyes (Mexico City: Centro de Investigaciones y Estudios Superiores en Antropología Social [CIESAS], 2001), 150, 296, 300.

22. Salvador Reyes Equiguas, "El huauhtli en la cultura náhuatl" (master's thesis, Universidad Nacional Autónoma de México, 2006), 88.

23. Reyes Equiguas, "El huauhtli," 89–91. The same concept of the image as a covering or skin exists in Maya culture, with the face and eyes possessing a power related to the supernatural realm: *B'aahil a'n.* See Erik Velázquez, "Naturaleza y papel de las personificaciones en los rituales mayas según las fuentes epigráficas, etnohistóricas y lexicográficas," in Andrés Ciudad Ruiz, Ma. Josefa Iglesias Ponce de León, and Miguel Sorroche Cuerva, eds., *El ritual en el mundo maya: De lo privado a lo público*

(Madrid: Sociedad Española de Estudios Mayas, 2010), 203–33.

24. A Nahua document written by a painters' guild uses "hacer aparecer" (make appear) and "hacer aparecer el *ixiptla*" (make the *ixiptla* appear), which refer to the image of something or someone, when describing a painting or a sculpture. *Anales de Juan Bautista,* 150, 296, 300.

25. Eduardo Viveiros de Castro, "Perspectivismo y multinaturalismo en la América indígena," in Adolfo Chaparro Amaya and Christian Shumacher, eds., *Racionalidad y discurso mítico* (Bogotá: Centro Editorial Universidad del Rosario, 2003), 212–13.

26. Viveiros de Castro, "Perspectivismo y multinaturalismo," 230.

27. Already in 1569, when Sahagún finished the version in Nahuatl, the Franciscans regarded spending money on scribes as going against their vow of poverty; thus, work on the book was suspended. López Austin, "Estudio introductorio," 1:43.

28. Sahagún, *Historia general* (2002), 1:62–63. English translation from "Sahagún's Prologues and Interpolations," 47.

29. Sherburne Cook and Woodrow Borah, *The Indian Population of Central Mexico, 1531–1610* (Berkeley: University of California Press, 1960).

30. Fray Bernardino de Sahagún, *Códice Florentino* [1575–77], Ms. Mediceo Palatino 220, fols. 389v and 390r, Biblioteca Medicea Laurenziana, Florence. English translation from "Sahagún's Prologues and Interpolations," 94.

31. Constantino Medina Lima, *Libro de los guardianes y los gobernadores de Cuauhtinchan (1519–1640)* (Mexico City: CIESAS, 1995), 57.

32. Paula Mues Orts, *La libertad del pincel: Los discursos sobre la nobleza de la pintura en Nueva España* (Mexico City: Universidad Iberoamericana, 2008), 37, 85, 171–229. Mues Orts confirms that Creole and mestizo painters in New Spain were interested in the pictorial debates among painters in Europe. It is highly possible that the indigenous painters were equally interested, although this phenomenon has not yet been studied.

33. Tom Cummins, "The Indulgent Image: Prints in the New World," in Ilona Katzew, ed., *Contested Visions in the Spanish Colonial World,* exh. cat. (Los Angeles: Los Angeles County Museum of Art, 2011), 203–25. Cummins shows engravings' importance in the creation of the new indigenous pictorial style in the Americas.

34. *Anales de Juan Bautista,* 27, 145, 191, 197.

35. Medina Lima, *Libro de los guardianes,* 41–43.

36. To reflect on "visual appropriations" by indigenous people in the context of the Renaissance and mestizo thought, see Serge Gruzinski, *La pensée métisse* (Paris: Fayard, 1999), 203–24. Translated by Deke Dusinberre as *The Mestizo Mind: The Intellectual Dynamics of Colonization and Globalization* (New York: Routledge, 2002).

37. Sahagún, *Florentine Codex,* book 11, p. 10.

38. On Renaissance categories of painting, see Michael Baxandall, *Painting and Experience in Fifteenth-Century Italy* (Oxford: Oxford University Press, 1988).

39. Fray Alonso de Molina, *Vocabulario en lengua castellana y mexicana* [1555–71], 3rd ed. (Mexico City: Porrúa, 1992), 122.

40. The imitation of nature was regarded as one of art's merits; it assimilated the idea of imitating Truth. This was the subject of considerable debate among artists and painting theoreticians in the Italian quattrocento. Baxandall, *Painting and Experience,* 140–41.

41. Baxandall, *Painting and Experience,* 29–103.

42. Gruzinski analyzes a similar painting that portrays a Mexican wolf; see his *La pensée métisse,* 214–17.

43. *Anales de Juan Bautista,* 199.

44. *Anales de Juan Bautista,* 150. The Nahuatl says: "quinexti yn ixiptlatzin tonantzin."

45. Miguel León-Portilla, *La filosofía náhuatl estudiada en sus fuentes,* 9th ed. (Mexico City: Universidad Nacional Autónoma de México, 2001), 66–67. In Nahuatl, *tlapalli* means both "red" and "colors" in general.

46. Berenice Alcántara Rojas introduced this concept to me in 2009. It has been more extensively developed in Diana Magaloni Kerpel, "The Traces of the Creative Process: Pictorial Materials and Techniques in the Beinecke Map," in Mary Miller and Barbara Mundy, eds., *Painting a Map of Sixteenth-Century Mexico City: Land, Writing, and Native Rule* (New Haven, Conn.: Yale University Press, 2012), 75–91.

47. Sahagún, *Florentine Codex,* book 11, p. 239.

48. Donald Robertson, *Mexican Manuscript Painting of the Early Colonial Period: The Metropolitan Schools* (Norman: University of Oklahoma Press, 1994), 171–72.

49. Gruzinski, *La pensée métisse,* 196–99.

50. [According to *Naturalis historia,* Apelles was an artist from ancient Greece, known for his paintings and for a lost treatise on the art of painting. –*Trans.*]

51. Jacob Isager, *Pliny on Art and Society: The Elder Pliny's Chapters on the History of Art* (New York: Routledge, 1991), 105–34.

52. Pliny the Elder, *Naturalis historia,* book 35, p. 50, cited by Isager, *Pliny on Art and Society,* 124–25.

53. Isager, *Pliny on Art and Society,* 105–34.

54. See notes 23 to 25.

55. Danièle Dehouve, "Nombrar los colores en náhuatl (siglos XVI–XX)," in Georges Roque, ed., *El color en el arte mexicano* (Mexico City: Universidad Nacional Autónoma de México, 2003), 101–20. The author notes that the luminosity of tones (lightness-darkness) is intrinsic to how colors are perceived and named in Nahuatl.

56. Sahagún, *Historia general* (2002), vol. 3, book 11, p. 1130.

57. Sahagún, *Florentine Codex,* book 11, p. 239.

58. Sahagún, *Historia general* (1979), fol. 372v.

59. Michelle P. Brown, *Understanding Illuminated Manuscripts: A Guide to Technical Terms* (Los Angeles: J. Paul Getty Museum, 1994), 16.

60. Garone Gravier, "Sahagún's Codex and Book Design," 196, identifies seven scribes, two of whom knew Latin, Spanish, and Nahuatl.

61.   This method of identifying the hands of artists, originally proposed by Giovanni Morelli, has been applied both to codices and to mural painting by important authors. See Carlo Ginzburg, "Morelli, Freud and Sherlock Holmes: Clues and Scientific Method," *History Workshop Journal,* no. 9 (1980): 5–36.

62.   The identification of artists was independent of the twenty portraits, but the proximity of the numbers is significant.

63.   Guilhem Olivier and Leonardo López Luján, "Images of Moctezuma and His Symbols of Power," in Colin McEwan and Leonardo López Luján, eds., *Moctezuma: Aztec Ruler,* exh. cat. (London: British Museum, 2009), 80–85.

64.   See notes 17, 21, 23, and 25.

65.   Louise Burkhart, "The Solar Christ in Nahuatl Doctrinal Texts of Early Colonial Mexico," *Ethnohistory* 35 (1988): 234–56.

66.   Susan Gillespie, *The Aztec Kings: The Construction of Rulership in Mexica History* (Tucson: University of Arizona Press, 1989), 136. The author discusses the fundamental concept of cyclic time in indigenous historiography, because the end of a cosmic era, also known as a "sun," had to coincide with the beginning of the new era. The painting reflects this concept.

67.   The studies of the identification of pigments and colorants were conducted by Dr. Piero Baglioni of the Consorzio per lo Sviluppo dei Sistemi a Grande Interfasi (CSGI) of the Università di Firenze and his team of scientists, with nondestructive methods of analysis: a handheld XRF spectrometer and Fourier Transform Infrared Spectrometer (FT-IR), both from Bruker Optics.

68.   The tones that we obtained in the experiments can be consulted in Piero Baglioni et al., "On the Nature of the Pigments," 79–105.

69.   On the widespread use of *achiote* (*achiotl*) as a pigment, see Elena Phipps, "Textile Colors and Colorants in the Andes," in Gerhard Wolf and Joseph Connors, eds., *Colors between Two Worlds: The* Florentine Codex *of Bernardino de Sahagún* (Florence: Kunsthistorisches Institut in Florenz, Max-Planck-Institut, 2011), 273–74.

70.   Sahagún, *Florentine Codex,* book 11, p. 241.

71.   Dibble and Anderson translate it as "red ochre" in Sahagún, *Florentine Codex,* book 11, p. 243.

72.   Alfredo López Austin, *Tamoanchan y Tlalocan* (Mexico City: Fondo de Cultura Económica, 1994), 23–29. Translated by Bernard R. Ortiz de Montellano and Thelma Ortiz de Montellano as *Tamoanchan, Tlalocan, Places of Mist* (Boulder: University Press of Colorado, 1997).

73.   Leonardo López Luján et al., "Línea y color en Tenochtitlán: Escultura policromada y pintura mural en el recinto sagrado de la capital mexica," *Estudios de cultura Náhuatl* 36 (2005): 18.

74.   López Austin, *Tamoanchan y Tlalocan,* 25–30; quotation from idem, *Tamoanchan, Tlalocan, Places of Mist,* 23.

75.   Sandra Zetina et al., "The Encoded Language of Herbs: Material Insights

into the *De la Cruz-Badiano Codex*," in Gerhard Wolf and Joseph Connors, eds., *Colors between Two Worlds: The* Florentine Codex *of Bernardino de Sahagún* (Florence: Kunsthistorisches Institut in Florenz, Max-Planck-Institut, 2011), 221–55. The authors studied the *De la Cruz-Badiano* manuscript, a Nahua medicinal herbarium made in the Real Colegio de Santa Cruz Tlatelolco. The plants represented generally have roots painted with minerals, while the flowers and leaves are made with colorants.

76.   Diana Magaloni Kerpel, "The Hidden Aesthetic of Red in the Painted Tombs of Oaxaca," *RES: Anthropology and Aesthetics* 57 (2010): 55–75.

77.   López Austin, *Tamoanchan y Tlalocan,* 25.

78.   Brown, *Understanding Illuminated Manuscripts,* 86.

79.   Sahagún, *Florentine Codex,* book 11, p. 240.

80.   Sahagún, *Florentine Codex,* book 1, pp. 29–30.

81.   Diana Magaloni Kerpel, "Images of the Beginning: The Painted Story of the Conquest of Mexico in Book XII of the *Florentine Codex*" (PhD diss., Yale University, 2004).

82.   Sahagún, *Historia general* (1979), vol. 3, book 12, fols. 446r–447v.

83.   Michel Graulich, *Myths from Ancient Mexico,* trans. Bernard R. Ortiz de Montellano and Thelma Ortiz de Montellano (Norman: University of Oklahoma Press, 1997), 91–95. Graulich proposes that those who were defeated in war were related to the light of the moon.

84.   Sahagún, *Florentine Codex,* book 11, p. 242.

85.   Olivier and López Luján, "Images of Moctezuma and His Symbols of Power," 78–122.

86.   Stephen Houston et al., *Veiled Brightness: A History of Ancient Maya Color* (Austin: University of Texas Press, 2009), 78–80.

87.   Representation of Moctezuma in Sahagún, *Códice Florentino,* Ms. Mediceo Palatino 219, book 7, fol. 3r, Biblioteca Medicea Laurenziana, Florence.

88.   López Austin, *Hombre-dios,* 119–20.

89.   Philippe-Alain Michaud, *Aby Warburg and the Image in Motion* (New York: Zone, 2004); and Giovanni Careri, "Aby Warburg: Rituel, *Pathosformel* et forme intermédiaire," in Carlo Severi, ed., "Image et anthropologie," special issue, *L'homme* 165 (2003): 41–76.

90.   Johannes Neurath, "Anacronismo, *pathos* y fantasma en los medios de expresión huicholes," in Elizabeth Araiza, ed., *Las artes del ritual: Nuevas propuestas para la antropología del arte desde el occidente de México* (Zamora, Mexico: Colegio de Michoacán, 2010), 104.

91.   This phenomenon takes place today with the creation of Huichol and Cora ritual masks. Changing the original designs counteracts the efficacy or danger embodied in masks, so it is safe to sell them to tourists. See Johannes Neurath, "Máscaras enmascaradas: Indígenas, mestizos, y dioses indígenas mestizos," *Relaciones internacionales* 26 (2005): 22–50.

92. Brown, *Understanding Illuminated Manuscripts,* 82.

93. Cipactli (Cayman Lord) and Tlaltecuhtli (Lord of the Earth) are used to name the earth goddess/god, a powerful being who has both genders.

94. We should recall that these gods played a role in the fall of Tollan and are also referred to at the fall of Mexico-Tenochtitlan in figure 14.

95. Fray Andrés de Olmos, *Historia de los mexicanos por sus pinturas* and [unknown author], *Histoire du méchique,* in Angel Ma. Garibay K., ed. and trans., *Teogonía e historia de los mexicanos: Tres opúsculos del siglo XVI* (Mexico City: Porrúa, 1965), 23–90, 91–120.

96. López Austin, *Tamoanchan y Tlalocan,* 92–101.

97. López Austin, *Tamoanchan y Tlalocan,* 100.

98. Alessandra Russo, *El realismo circular: Tierras, espacios, y paisajes de la cartografía indígena novohispana, siglos XVI y XVII* (Mexico City: Universidad Nacional Autónoma de México, 2005), 87–88.

99. For more on the significance of the number eight in Christianity and in the Nahua worldview, see Martha Fernández, *La imagen del Templo de Jerusalén en la Nueva España* (Mexico City: Universidad Nacional Autónoma de México, 2003), 43–44, 56–61, 127–35; and David Freidel, Linda Schele, and Joy Parker, *Maya Cosmos: Three Thousand Years on the Shaman's Path* (New York: William Morrow, 1993), 72–73.

100. Fernández, *La imagen del Templo de Jerusalén en la Nueva España.*

101. Sahagún, *Florentine Codex,* book 7, p. 13.

102. Sahagún, *Florentine Codex,* book 4, p. 27.

103. Sahagún, *Florentine Codex,* book 7, p. 13.

104. López Austin, *Tamoanchan y Tlalocan,* 25.

105. Sahagún, *Florentine Codex,* book 11, p. 240.

106. Isager, *Pliny on Art and Society,* 76–79.

107. Berenice Alcántara Rojas, "*In Nepapan Xochitl*: The Power of Flowers in the Works of Sahagún," in Gerhard Wolf and Joseph Connors, eds., *Colors between Two Worlds: The* Florentine Codex *of Bernardino de Sahagún* (Florence: Kunthistorisches Institut in Florenz, Max-Planck-Institut, 2011), 107–32.

108. López Austin, *Tamoanchan y Tlalocan,* 46; quotations from idem, *Tamoanchan, Tlalocan, Places of Mist,* 52.

109. López Austin, *Tamoanchan y Tlalocan,* 92; quotation from idem, *Tamoanchan, Tlalocan, Places of Mist,* 110.

110. López Austin, *Tamoanchan y Tlalocan,* 92; quotation from idem, *Tamoanchan, Tlalocan, Places of Mist,* 110.

BIBLIOGRAPHY OF SELECTED WORKS

Alcántara Rojas, Berenice. "*In Nepapan Xochitl:* The Power of Flowers in the Works of Sahagún." In Gerhard Wolf and Joseph Connors, eds., *Colors between Two Worlds: The* Florentine Codex *of Bernardino de Sahagún,* 107–32. Florence: Kunsthistorisches Institut in Florenz, Max-Planck-Institut, 2011.

Anderson, Arthur J. O. "Sahagún's Prologues and Interpolations." In Fray Bernardino de Sahagún, *Florentine Codex: General History of the Things of New Spain,* part 1, *Introduction and Indices,* 45–101. Translated by Arthur J. O. Anderson and Charles E. Dibble. Santa Fe, N.Mex.: School of American Research, 1950–69. Reprint, Salt Lake City: University of Utah Press, 1970–82.

———. "Variations on a Sahaguntine Theme." In Fray Bernardino de Sahagún, *Florentine Codex: General History of the Things of New Spain,* part 1, *Introduction and Indices,* 3–29. Translated by Arthur J. O. Anderson and Charles E. Dibble. Santa Fe, N.Mex.: School of American Research, 1950–69. Reprint, Salt Lake City: University of Utah Press, 1970–82.

Baglioni, Piero, et al. "On the Nature of the Pigments of the *General History of the Things of New Spain: The Florentine Codex.*" In Gerhard Wolf and Joseph Connors, eds., *Colors between Two Worlds: The* Florentine Codex *of Bernardino de Sahagún,* 79–105. Florence: Kunsthistorisches Institut in Florenz, Max-Planck-Institut, 2011.

Baxandall, Michael. *Painting and Experience in Fifteenth-Century Italy.* 2nd ed. Oxford: Oxford University Press, 1988.

Brown, Michelle P. *Understanding Illuminated Manuscripts: A Guide to Technical Terms.* Los Angeles: J. Paul Getty Museum, 1994.

Burkhart, Louise. "The Solar Christ in Nahuatl Doctrinal Texts of Early Colonial Mexico." *Ethnohistory* 35 (1988): 234–56.

Careri, Giovanni. "Aby Warburg: Rituel, *Pathosformel* et forme intermédiaire." In Carlo Severi, ed., "Image et anthropologie," special issue, *L'homme* 165 (2003): 41–76.

Cook, Sherburne, and Woodrow Borah. *The Indian Population of Central Mexico, 1531–1610.* Berkeley: University of California Press, 1960.

Cummins, Tom. "The Indulgent Image: Prints in the New World." In Ilona Katzew, ed., *Contested Visions in the Spanish Colonial World,* 203–25. Exh. cat. Los Angeles: Los Angeles County Museum of Art, 2011.

Dackerman, Susan. *Painted Prints: The Revelation of Color in Northern Renaissance and Baroque Engravings, Etchings and Woodcuts.* Exh. cat. University Park: Pennsylvania State University Press, 2002.

Dehouve, Danièle. "Nombrar los colores en náhuatl (siglos XVI–XX)." In Georges Roque, ed., *El color en el arte mexicano*, 101–20. Mexico City: Universidad Nacional Autónoma de México, 2003.

Díaz, Gisele, and Alan Rodgers. *The Codex Borgia: A Full-Color Restoration of the Ancient Mexican Manuscript.* New York: Dover, 1993.

Escalante, Pablo. *Los códices mesoamericanos antes y después de la conquista española: Historia de un lenguaje pictográfico.* Mexico City: Fondo de Cultura Económica, 2010.

Fernández, Martha. *La imagen del Templo de Jerusalén en la Nueva España.* Mexico City: Universidad Nacional Autónoma de México, 2003.

Freidel, David, Linda Schele, and Joy Parker. *Maya Cosmos: Three Thousand Years on the Shaman's Path.* New York: William Morrow, 1993.

Garone Gravier, Marina. "Sahagún's Codex and Book Design in the Indigenous Context." In Gerhard Wolf and Joseph Connors, eds., *Colors between Two Worlds: The* Florentine Codex *of Bernardino de Sahagún,* 157–97. Florence: Kunsthistorisches Institut in Florenz, Max-Planck-Institut, 2011.

Gillespie, Susan. *The Aztec Kings: The Construction of Rulership in Mexica History.* Tucson: The University of Arizona Press, 1989.

Ginzburg, Carlo. "Morelli, Freud and Sherlock Holmes: Clues and Scientific Method." *History Workshop Journal,* no. 9 (1980): 5–36.

Graulich, Michel. *Myths from Ancient Mexico.* Translated by Bernard R. Ortiz de Montellano and Thelma Ortiz de Montellano. Norman: University of Oklahoma Press, 1997.

Gruzinski, Serge. *La pensée métisse.* Paris: Fayard, 1999. Translated by Deke Dusinberre as *The Mestizo Mind: The Intellectual Dynamics of Colonization and Globalization.* New York: Routledge, 2002.

Hernández de León-Portilla, Ascensión. "La historia general de Sahagún a la luz de las enciclopedias de la tradición greco-romana." In Miguel León-Portilla, ed., *Bernardino de Sahagún: Quinientos años de presencia,* 41–60. Mexico City: Universidad Nacional Autónoma de México, 2002.

Histoire du méchique. In Angel Ma. Garibay K., ed. and trans., *Teogonía e historia de los mexicanos: Tres opúsculos del siglo XVI,* 91–120. Mexico City: Porrúa, 1965.

Houston, Stephen, et al. *Veiled Brightness: A History of Ancient Maya Color.* Austin: University of Texas Press, 2009.

Isager, Jacob. *Pliny on Art and Society: The Elder Pliny's Chapters on the History of Art.* New York: Routledge, 1991.

León-Portilla, Miguel. *La filosofía náhuatl estudiada en sus fuentes.* 9th ed. Mexico City: Universidad Nacional Autónoma de México, 1959. Reprint, Mexico City: Universidad Nacional Autónoma de México, 2001.

López Austin, Alfredo. "Estudio introductorio a Bernardino de Sahagún." In Fray Bernardino de Sahagún, *Historia general de las cosas de Nueva España,* 1:37–52. Edited and with an introduction, glossary, and notes by Alfredo López Austin and Josefina García Quintana. Mexico City: Conaculta, 2002.

———. *Hombre-dios: Religión y política en el mundo náhuatl.* Mexico City: Universidad Nacional Autónoma de México, 1973.

———. *Tamoanchan y Tlalocan.* Mexico City: Fondo de Cultura Económica, 1994. Translated by Bernard R. Ortiz de Montellano and Thelma Ortiz de Montellano as *Tamoanchan, Tlalocan, Places of Mist.* Boulder: University Press of Colorado, 1997.

López Luján, Leonardo, et al. "Línea y color en Tenochtitlán: Escultura policromada y pintura mural en el recinto sagrado de la capital mexica." *Estudios de cultura Náhuatl* 36 (2005): 15–43.

Magaloni Kerpel, Diana. "The Hidden Aesthetic of Red in the Painted Tombs of Oaxaca." *RES: Anthropology and Aesthetics* 57 (2010)*:* 55–75.

———. "History under the Rainbow: The Conquest of Mexico in the *Florentine Codex.*" In Ilona Katzew, ed., *Contested Visions in the Spanish Colonial World,* 79–95. Los Angeles: Los Angeles County Museum of Art, 2011.

———. "Images of the Beginning: The Painted Story of the Conquest of Mexico in Book XII of the *Florentine Codex.*" PhD diss., Yale University, 2004.

———. "Painters of the New World: The Process of Making the *Florentine Codex.*" In Gerhard Wolf and Joseph Connors, eds., *Colors between Two Worlds: The* Florentine Codex *of Bernardino de Sahagún,* 47–76. Florence: Kunsthistorisches Institut in Florenz, Max-Planck-Institut, 2011.

———. "The Traces of the Creative Process: Pictorial Materials and Techniques in the Beinecke Map." In Mary Miller and Barbara Mundy, eds., *Painting a Map of Sixteenth-Century Mexico City: Land, Writing, and Native Rule,* 75–91. New Haven, Conn.: Yale University Press, 2012.

Markey, Lia. " 'Istoria della terra chiamata la nuova spagna'*:* The History and Reception of Sahagún's Codex at the Medici Court." In Gerhard Wolf and Joseph Connors, eds., *Colors between Two Worlds: The* Florentine Codex *of Bernardino de Sahagún,* 199–218. Florence: Kunsthistorisches Institut in Florenz, Max-Planck-Institut, 2011.

Martínez Rodríguez, José Luis. *El Códice Florentino y la historia general de Sahagún.* Mexico City: Archivo General de la Nación, 1982.

Medina Lima, Constantino. *Libro de los guardianes y los gobernadores de Cuauhtinchan (1519-1640).* Mexico City: Centro de Investigaciones y Estudios Superiores en Antropología Social (CIESAS), 1995.

Michaud, Philippe-Alain. *Aby Warburg and the Image in Motion.* New York: Zone, 2004.

Molina, Alonso de. *Vocabulario en lengua castellana y mexicana* [1555-71]. 3rd ed. Mexico City: Porrúa, 1992.

Motolinía, Toribio de Benavente. *Historia de los indios de la Nueva España.* Mexico City: Porrúa, 1990.

Mues Orts, Paula. *La libertad del pincel: Los discursos sobre la nobleza de la pintura en Nueva España.* Mexico City: Universidad Iberoamericana, 2008.

Neurath, Johannes. "Anacronismo, *pathos* y fantasma en los medios de expresión huicholes." In Elizabeth Araiza, ed., *Las artes del ritual: Nuevas propuestas para la antropología del arte desde el occidente de México,* 99-125. Zamora, Mexico: Colegio de Michoacán, 2010.

———. "Máscaras enmascaradas: Indígenas, mestizos y dioses indígenas mestizos." *Relaciones internacionales* 26 (2005): 22-50.

Olivier, Guilhem, and Leonardo López Luján. "Images of Moctezuma and His Symbols of Power." In Colin McEwan and Leonardo López Luján, eds., *Moctezuma: Aztec Ruler,* 78-123. Exh. cat. London: The British Museum, 2009.

Olmos, Fray Andrés de. *Historia de los mexicanos por sus pinturas.* In Angel Ma. Garibay K., ed. and trans., *Teogonía e historia de los mexicanos: Tres opúsculos del siglo XVI,* 23-90. Mexico City: Porrúa, 1965.

Phipps, Elena. "Textile Colors and Colorants in the Andes." In Gerhard Wolf and Joseph Connors, eds., *Colors between Two Worlds: The* Florentine Codex *of Bernardino de Sahagún,* 257-80. Florence: Kunsthistorisches Institut in Florenz, Max-Planck-Institut, 2011.

Reyes, Luis, trans. *Los anales de Juan Bautista.* Mexico City: Centro de Investigaciones y Estudios Superiores en Antropología Social (CIESAS), 2001.

Reyes Equiguas, Salvador. "El huauhtli en la cultura náhuatl." Master's thesis, Universidad Nacional Autónoma de México, 2006.

Robertson, Donald. *Mexican Manuscript Painting of the Early Colonial Period: The Metropolitan Schools.* Norman: University of Oklahoma Press, 1994.

Romero Galván, José Rubén. "Fray Bernardino de Sahagún y la historia general de las cosas de Nueva España." In Miguel León-Portilla, ed., *Bernardino de Sahagún: Quinientos años de presencia,* 29-40. Mexico City: Universidad Nacional Autónoma de México, 2002.

Russo, Alessandra. *El realismo circular: Tierras, espacios y paisajes de la cartografía indígena novohispana, siglos XVI y XVII.* Mexico City: Universidad Nacional Autónoma de México, 2005.

Sahagún, Fray Bernardino de. *Códice Florentino.* Ms. Mediceo Palatino 218, 219, 220 (1575-77). Biblioteca Medicea Laurenziana, Florence.

———. *Florentine Codex: General History of the Things of New Spain.* Translated by Arthur J. O. Anderson and Charles E. Dibble. 13 vols. Santa Fe, N.Mex.: School of American Research, 1950-69. Reprint, Salt Lake City: University of Utah Press, 1970-82.

———. *Historia general de las cosas de Nueva España.* Edited and with an introduction, glossary, and notes by Alfredo López Austin and Josefina García Quintana. 3 vols. Mexico City: Conaculta, 2002.

———. *Historia general de las cosas de Nueva España.* Facsimile. 3 vols. Mexico City: Secretaría de Gobernación, 1979.

Velázquez, Erik. "Naturaleza y papel de las personificaciones en los rituales mayas según las fuentes epigráficas, etnohistóricas y lexicográficas." In Andrés Ciudad Ruiz, Ma. Josefa Iglesias Ponce de León, and Miguel Sorroche Cuerva, eds., *El ritual en el mundo maya: De lo privado a lo público,* 203-34. Madrid: Sociedad Española de Estudios Mayas, 2010.

Viveiros de Castro, Eduardo. "Perspectivismo y multinaturalismo en la América indígena." In Adolfo Chaparro Amaya and Christian Shumacher, eds., *Racionalidad y discurso mítico,* 191-243. Bogotá: Centro Editorial Universidad del Rosario, 2003.

Zetina, Sandra, et al., "The Encoded Language of Herbs: Material Insights into the *De la Cruz-Badiano Codex.*" In Gerhard Wolf and Joseph Connors, eds., *Colors between Two Worlds: The* Florentine Codex *of Bernardino de Sahagún,* 221-55. Florence: Kunsthistorisches Institut in Florenz, Max-Planck-Institut, 2011.

This book was made possible thanks to the generous help of Piero Baglioni; without his support I could not have undertaken the research. I am grateful to my professors, because their teachings have come to form the basis of this work: Beatriz de la Fuente, Miguel León-Portilla, Alfredo López Austin, Eduardo Matos, Mary E. Miller, and Teresa Uriarte. I am also grateful for the inspiration and support of colleagues and friends who influenced my work: Manuel Aguilar, Berenice Alcántara, Pablo Amador, Pedro Ángeles Jiménez, Clara Bargellini, Claudia Brittenham, Johanna Broda, Louise Burkhart, Davíd Carrasco, David Chelazzi, Jaime Cuadriello, Tom Cummins, Karen Dakin, Alberto Díaz, Ana Díaz, Patricia Díaz, Lilia Félix, Laura Filloy, Rodorico Giorgi, Liliana Giorgulli, Serge Gruzinski, Arturo León, Leonardo López Luján, Cuauhtémoc Medina, Barbara Mundy, Federico Navarrete, Johannes Neurath, Jay Oles, Guilhem Olivier, Francesco Pellizzi, Ernesto Peñaloza, José Luis Pérez, Joanne Pillsbury, Giovanna Rao, Salvador Reyes, Alessandra Russo, José Luis Ruvalcaba, Durdica Segota, Dora Sierra, Ignacio Silva, Rafael Tena, Kevin Terraciano, Erik Velázquez, Gerhard Wolf, and Sandra Zetina. I dedicate this book to Maia, Kira, and Michael.

Diana Magaloni Kerpel

DIANA MAGALONI KERPEL holds a PhD in art history from Yale University. She is the director of the program for the Art of the Ancient Americas at the Los Angeles County Museum of Art and was previously the director of the Museo Nacional de Antropología in Mexico City. Magaloni Kerpel has also worked for many years at the Instituto de Investigaciones Estéticas at the Universidad Nacional Autónoma de México (UNAM), where her research has focused on the documentation, conservation, and study of pre-Hispanic Mexican murals. The results of her research have been published in such journals as *RES: Anthropology and Aesthetics* and *Artes de México,* as well as in numerous books, including *Contested Visions in the Spanish Colonial World* (2011), *Colors between Two Worlds: The* Florentine Codex *of Bernardino de Sahagún* (2012), and *Painting a Map of Sixteenth-Century Mexico City: Land, Writing, and Native Rule* (2012).

CUAUHTÉMOC MEDINA is head curator at the Museo Universitario Arte Contemporáneo (MUAC) at UNAM. In 2012, he was the curator of the Manifesta 9 biennial in Genk, Belgium, titled *The Deep of the Modern,* in association with Katerina Gregos and Dawn Ades. Medina received the 2012 Walter Hopps Award for Curatorial Achievement.

Brian Sweeney, Council Chair
Joel A. Aronowitz
Catherine Benkaim
Denise Decker
Tom Decker
Beverly Denenberg
Stuart Denenberg
Florence Fearrington
Arthur Greenberg
Richard Kelton
Wynnsan Moore
Tania N. Norris
Anna Oberwelland
Timm Oberwelland
Monique Owen
Tony Owen
Lynda Resnick
Stewart Resnick
Richard Rosenthal
Strawn Rosenthal
Richard A. Simms
Eva Sweeney
Barbara Timmer
Carolyn Wellisz
Tadeusz Wellisz

OTHER BOOKS
PUBLISHED BY
THE GETTY RESEARCH
INSTITUTE

The Aztec Calendar Stone
Edited by Khristaan D. Villela and Mary Ellen Miller
Introduction by Khristaan D. Villela, Matthew H. Robb, and Mary Ellen Miller
ISBN 978-1-60606-004-9 (hardcover)

*China on Paper: European and Chinese Works from the
Late Sixteenth to the Early Nineteenth Century*
Edited by Marcia Reed and Paola Demattè
ISBN 978-1-60606-068-1 (paper)

Display & Art History: The Düsseldorf Gallery and Its Catalogue
Thomas W. Gaehtgens and Louis Marchesano
ISBN 978-1-60606-092-6 (paper)

*The Getty Murúa: Essays on the Making of Martín de Murúa's
"Historia General del Piru," J. Paul Getty Museum Ms. Ludwig XIII 16*
Edited by Thomas B. F. Cummins and Barbara Anderson
ISBN 978-0-89236-894-5 (hardcover)

Modern Japanese Art and the Meiji State: The Politics of Beauty
Dōshin Satō
Translated by Hiroshi Nara
ISBN 978-1-60606-059-9 (hardcover)

*Printing the Grand Manner: Charles Le Brun and Monumental Prints
in the Age of Louis XIV*
Louis Marchesano and Christian Michel
ISBN 978-0-89236-980-5 (hardcover)